SPEAK WITH POWER AND CONFIDENCE

SPEAK WITH POWER AND CONFIDENCE

TESTED IDEAS FOR BECOMING A MORE POWERFUL COMMUNICATOR

Patrick Collins
author of *Negotiate to Win!*

STERLING

New York / London
www.sterlingpublishing.com

STERLING and the distinctive Sterling logo are registered trademarks
of Sterling Publishing Co., Inc.

Library of Congress Cataloging-in-Publication Data

Collins, Patrick J.
  Speak with power and confidence : tested ideas for becoming a more powerful
communicator / Patrick Collins.
     p. cm.
  Rev. ed. of: Say it with power and confidence. c1998.
  Includes bibliographical references and index.
  ISBN 978-1-4027-6123-2
  1. Public speaking. I. Collins, Patrick J. Say it with power and confidence. II. Title.
  PN4121.C613 2009
  808.5'1—dc22

                                                          2008036175

10 9 8 7 6 5 4 3 2 1

Published by Sterling Publishing Co., Inc.
387 Park Avenue South, New York, NY 10016
© 2009 by Patrick Collins
Distributed in Canada by Sterling Publishing
C/o Canadian Manda Group, 165 Dufferin Street
Toronto, Ontario, Canada M6K 3H6
Distributed in the United Kingdom by GMC Distribution Services
Castle Place, 166 High Street, Lewes, East Sussex, England BN7 1XU
Distributed in Australia by Capricorn Link (Australia) Pty. Ltd.
P.O. Box 704, Windsor, NSW 2756, Australia

Sterling ISBN 978-1-4027-6123-2

Previously published in 1998 by Prentice Hall, Paramus, New Jersey,
under the title *Say It with Power and Confidence.*

For information about custom editions, special sales, premium and
corporate purchases, please contact Sterling Special Sales
Department at 800-805-5489 or specialsales@sterlingpublishing.com.

For Donna, Kristen, and Lauren

Contents

Introduction

Why You Need *Speak with Power and Confidence*

If you have ever left a meeting, a sales presentation, or even a job interview thinking, "It could have gone better," or "The *next* time they ask me that question, I'll say . . . ," you need this book. *Speak with Power and Confidence* can help you get your audience back—whether your audience is one person or one hundred.

As skilled as you might be in some aspects of your life, you are probably at a disadvantage when it comes to getting your message across with confidence, authority, and credibility in order to get what you want from an interpersonal encounter. *Speak with Power and Confidence* is a comprehensive guide to giving you the communicative edge—the advantage in every situation from the speaker's podium to the conference room, and beyond.

The need to be a truly powerful communicator is greater than ever before. In this era of corporate downsizing, being an *essential* member of the team is a major key to survival. Strong interpersonal skills are the main ingredient in your personal survival kit. *Speak with Power and Confidence* can help you build the skills that will help make you a key member of any team.

The art of masterful communication is now a greater challenge than ever. There was a time when an adequate performance at the speaker's podium was enough. That's no longer the case. Today you must function in multiple areas: the boardroom, the TV studio, and even the witness stand. *Speak with Power and Confidence* will give you the information and specific tactics you need—not just to *survive*, but to *prosper* in all public-speaking scenarios.

If you feel a sense of inadequacy as a communicator, you are not alone. Even if you are the beneficiary of a lengthy and rigorous education, you may also be its victim. That's because the spoken word, in spite of its impact and power on all of our lives, is still a fleeting event, virtually impossible to measure or evaluate. Therefore, educators, whose every success or failure is reflected by student performance on standardized tests, have largely ignored interpersonal skills. Sadly, such essentials as how to captivate people with your ideas are still excluded from most curricula. *Speak with Power and Confidence* will remedy that deficit.

How *Speak with Power and Confidence* Can Help You

Even after nearly thirty years as a communications educator and consultant, I still marvel at the obvious and costly communicative blunders made by people who should know better. As the chair of an academic department, I have watched highly educated people effectively demolish their chances of success in a job interview with a single, needlessly errant, response. In helping senior executives prepare for major addresses, I have seen normally clear-thinking, well-intentioned people bore, alienate, or even offend the very people they wanted to touch with their message. I have seen executives in the midst of a crisis make the disastrous miscalculation of failing to communicate their actions.

Over the years, seeing so many people fail to achieve their communicative objectives in so many crucial situations, I sought to develop ways to help people I worked with and taught, not by burying them in theory, but by developing specific and practical means of avoiding the communicative pitfalls that surround them. *Speak with Power and Confidence* is the result of that effort. It is a book designed to give you the advantage in nearly *every* communicative situation you will encounter.

Speak with Power and Confidence provides a unique combination of tips, tactics, and advice you can apply right away on the path to becoming a more powerful communicator. For example, you'll learn how to:

- Send just the right nonverbal signals in any situation
- Minimize anxiety and maximize self-confidence
- Be an effective public speaker—even if you hate public speaking!

• Use language to get and keep people on your side
• Handle tough audiences and tough questions in any setting
• Avoid common blunders in the job interview
• Get your message across to the media
... and much more!

All the information in *Speak with Power and Confidence* is presented in a direct, no-nonsense style so that you can begin applying it immediately and get results. Each chapter begins with an at-a-glance summary to let you know what's covered and ends with a list of specific techniques for review. *Speak with Power and Confidence* is a book you will not only want to read from cover to cover, but will also want to use as a reference and guide through the verbal minefields we all face from time to time.

How *Speak with Power and Confidence* Is Organized

There are three elements in any communicative encounter that can maximize your chances of success if you manage them well—You, the Message, and the Situation. *Speak with Power and Confidence* examines each of these elements and shows you how to manage them so you will gain the communicative advantage in virtually every encounter.

Part One: Maximizing Your Personal Communicative Power

Chapter 1 of *Speak with Power and Confidence* is about *you*—that is, about the signals you send before you even say a word. You'll learn how body language, eyes, gestures, and even silence can help you gain the upper hand. You'll learn how to improve the variety and quality of your voice—an important part of making just the right impression on your listeners. Anxiety is a formidable obstacle preventing many people from attaining their goals. If you're one of the many people who would rather face death than speak in public, you'll learn how to manage your anxiety and build greater self-confidence in all your interpersonal encounters.

IMPROVING YOUR LANGUAGE POWER An extremely important part of any message is the language you choose to get your point across. The right choices will dramatically increase the impact of your message, whereas a few wrong choices will make your audience members tune you out. Chapter 2 tells you what you need to know to make the right choices. Which is more effective—formal or conversational language? How do you deliver highly technical material and still keep things interesting? How do you make your spoken words more colorful? More memorable? These are just a few of the questions answered in Chapter 2.

LISTENING—THE FORGOTTEN SIDE OF COMMUNICATION Studies have found that we remember less than 10 percent of what we hear. That's because we can process information faster than anyone can talk. If you retain more of the information you hear, you'll have the edge whenever it's important to get all the information you can.

In Chapter 3, "Becoming a Better Listener," you'll learn how to break down the perceptual barriers that cause you to tune people out even when their message is worthwhile. You'll also discover ways to eliminate distractions and improve your listening environment. Applying these valuable listening tips will mean a dramatic increase in the amount of information you retain and use to your advantage.

Part Two: Preparing and Delivering
Powerful Speeches and Presentations

Effective communication skills will make people take notice of what you have to say.

Chapter 4 of *Speak with Power and Confidence*, "Speechwriting: How to Create a Powerful Message," takes you through a step-by-step method of showcasing your ideas to make them more memorable. No one listens to every word you say, but this chapter will show you how to hold an audience's interest and how to really grab their attention at crucial points in your message.

MAKING SURE YOUR MESSAGE HITS HOME The failure to tailor your message to your audience is a fatal mistake that many communicators make, from public speakers to media guests. Chapter 5 teaches you how to reach out to your particular audience and includes a section on special tactics for highly educated or sophisticated audiences. This chapter even provides tips for effective communication in a "politically correct" environment, with advice on issues of race, gender, and ethnicity.

HANDLING TOUGH QUESTIONS AND TOUGH AUDIENCES The most carefully crafted and delivered address is worthless if you can't handle the audience questions that are likely to follow. Chapter 6 of *Speak with Power and Confidence* shows you not only how to field questions from an audience but also, and more important, how to handle the tough questions that can follow your presentation. Q&A skills are the basis for a wide array of crucial communicative situations, from the media interview to the Q&A period that follows a speech, to the job interview and even the witness stand. This chapter shows you how to take control without seeming to be controlling, how to respond to "trick" questions, how to stall for time without making it obvious, and even how to handle the potentially awkward moment when you have to say "I don't know."

THE SALES PRESENTATION Sales presentations are really public-speaking contests in which the individual or team with the best presentation get the prize: the account. Having the best product or service often has little to do with the outcome.

Chapter 7, "Making Effective Sales Presentations," helps you and your team deliver the best presentation every time. You'll learn to avoid the common errors made even by those who consider themselves old pros, who often stumble when treading the delicate ground of how to seem aggressive and direct without turning customers off and how to talk about the competition bluntly without offending anyone. Chapter 7 also includes tips on mastering the language of winning, as well as ideas on how to manage team presentations effectively.

SPUR-OF-THE-MOMENT AND SPECIAL-OCCASION SPEECHES We all admire people who seem to be able to speak at a moment's notice on almost any subject and who somehow manage to come up with remarks that most of us consider not only adequate but bordering on eloquent. The operative word here is "seem," as successful spontaneous speaking is anything but spontaneous. These apparently gifted orators are actually using a few tricks that are revealed in Chapter 8 so that you can function with equal brilliance on the spur of the moment. Chapter 8 provides the information and tips you'll need to shine at special and seemingly spontaneous moments like tributes, award acceptances, nominations, toasts, and even eulogies.

Part Three: Surefire Strategies for Special Situations

THE JOB INTERVIEW With the possible exception of the public-speaking invitation and the tax audit, no other situation inspires as much agony as the job interview. Chapter 9, "The Job Interview," is about maximizing your chances of success in this all-important quest. It also provides guidance on what to do if things don't go your way.

Beginning with the vital pre-interview steps that most job candidates ignore, you'll start to build your advantage even before the interview takes place. Along with an extensive section of sample questions, this chapter tells you the *real* meaning behind often-asked questions.

There are also sample correct and incorrect responses designed to give you highly specific information on what you should and shouldn't say. You'll even learn to handle questions that are intended to see how you deal with stress, and you'll also learn how to handle the all-important but delicate issue of how to talk about salary requirements.

HANDLING THE MEDIA Chapter 10, "Handling the Media," gives you the tactical material you'll need to make a credible and comfortable on-air appearance. Included is valuable information about how to control the agenda and get your point across in any media interview. You'll learn specific techniques for getting the most out of the various kinds of interviews: in-studio, remote camera, and even the "ambush" interview. In case you're new to the TV studio, you'll also find enough technical information (including how to know which camera to look at) to put you at ease. There is even a section on call-in radio shows.

While the emphasis is on electronic (radio and TV) journalists, print reporters present another set of problems and opportunities. Chapter 10 shows you how to get the best coverage from a more casual, lengthy, and *potentially dangerous* print interview.

THE WITNESS STAND   With the ever-increasing number of civil cases filed annually, as well as the thousands of legislative and regulatory hearings, you are more and more likely to find yourself on the witness stand. In this adversarial setting, you can expect the opposition to be ready with some tricks and traps to take you in some informational direction you'd rather not go. Chapter 11, "Preparing to Be an Effective Witness," arms you with strategies to avoid being taken advantage of by the other side. You'll discover such valuable tactics as how to spot hidden messages in your counsel's objection and how to maintain your comfort and credibility on the witness stand.

CRISIS COMMUNICATION   Those who have been through any kind of corporate crisis will tell you that the worst time to start planning how you'll handle things is in the midst of a crisis. Chapter 12, "Handling Crisis Communications," is a guide to formulating a crisis communication plan.

Included is such vital information as (1) defining the crisis, (2) getting the most from your PR and legal advisers, (3) media planning for the crisis, (4) the importance of symbolic communication, and (5) communicating successful recovery. You'll find this chapter extremely helpful in tackling the communicative aspects of a crisis, especially if you apply its contents *before* things have "hit the fan."

CONDUCTING SUCCESSFUL MEETINGS If people want to assess your ability as a manager or executive, there is no need to dig out your personnel file. All they have to do is watch you run a meeting. Are things getting done? Moving along? Falling apart? At no time is your ability to manage more visible or more vulnerable than when you run a meeting. Yet little information is available on precisely how to proceed when you're thrown into this potentially risky setting.

Speak with Power and Confidence fills this information gap with a unique chapter containing all you'll need to know to handle meetings like a seasoned veteran and master parliamentarian. In Chapter 13, you'll gain vital information on how to control the content and tone of meetings, how to set the level of formality, and how to use rules to your advantage. You'll also learn effective techniques for holding elections, a tricky and sometimes explosive piece of business.

But meeting aren't just about issues; they are also about managing people. That's why this chapter shows you how to prevent meetings from degenerating into gripe sessions and how to handle conflict between those present.

TWENTY-SEVEN QUICK FIXES TO ENHANCE COMMUNICATIVE POWER *Speak with Power and Confidence* is intended to be the most comprehensive book of its kind, giving you all the information you need to build dramatic and tangible gains in your ability to communicate in a wide array of situations. The summary in Chapter 14 contains a compilation of the trickiest skills to master, as well as a comprehensive list of the most costly errors you are likely to make. This chapter, which covers tips on everything from the speaker's podium to the media interview, should jog your memory about important points covered earlier. It is also offered as a kind of communicative pep talk, an intensive lightning round review of the essentials that will make you a powerful and confident communicator.

PART ONE

MAXIMIZING YOUR PERSONAL COMMUNICATIVE POWER

CHAPTER ONE

Developing Nonverbal Communication Skills

AT-A-GLANCE SUMMARY

Most of this book is about helping you to get your message across and accomplishing your communicative agenda. This chapter, however, is about you.

Audiences decide whether to accept or reject your message from the moment you enter a room, gathering impressions about you and your message by observing everything from body language and facial expressions to eye contact and voice. How you handle these nonverbal factors ("signal behaviors") can make or break your performance.

This chapter provides the information you need to manage your signal behaviors so you'll have the edge in all the communicative situations discussed in this book, from the speaker's podium to the broadcast studio and from the negotiating table to the witness stand.

The communication process begins as soon as you enter the room, whether it's for an audience of one in a job interview or for a gathering of hundreds at the annual shareholders meeting.

Sending the Right Nonverbal Signals

Your signal behaviors are an integral part of every verbal encounter. Voice, gestures, eye contact, body language, and even your appearance can help, or in some cases hinder, your impact on an audience.

If you mismanage your signal behaviors, you will lack the power and impact you could and should have. You risk coming across as somewhere between boring and arrogant, uncaring or incompetent, and generally worthy of little more than an audience's polite tolerance.

If you don't have a high opinion of your communicative skills, let me provide you with some encouraging news: I have worked with thousands of speakers over the years, and I have yet to meet one who does *everything* poorly. For example, those with superior verbal skills might not shine when it comes to vocal expressiveness, but none of the speakers I've met were in need of a total "communicative makeover."

As you use the techniques in this chapter, don't put together an "act." It will only come apart under pressure. Instead, concentrate on making some gradual adjustments in your signal behaviors as needed, while working with and building on your strengths. This way you'll come across as both comfortable and consistent—two sure hallmarks of an effective, credible spokesperson.

Now let's look at the major signal behaviors and how you can use them to boost the impact of your spoken word.

Presenting a Commanding Entrance

If you're giving a speech, your entrance and the first moment at the podium should be smooth and seamless, with a minimal but definite moment to adjust the microphone, arrange your notes, and establish your comfort level.

If you skip this step, your speech will be disjointed and won't flow as freely as you'd like. The result? The audience will see a speaker who is anxious and "a bit off," and wonder why. If your entrance isn't commanding, you'll immediately lose credibility and authority.

How do you smooth out an entrance and make sure that the all-important first moment goes smoothly? *Manage the environment!*

Any time you're giving a presentation, testifying at a hearing, or appearing on a TV program, get there with enough time to check out the surroundings, even the day before for a particularly important event.

Whenever necessary, have changes made in advance, be it a taller podium, a better microphone, or a rearrangement of the chairs. If you're going to be using a flip chart, make sure there are markers and that they work. Even if you arrive early just to become familiar with the surroundings, you'll make yourself more comfortable by doing so and prepare yourself to make a commanding entrance.

The comfort and psychological advantage you gain by being familiar with the speaking environment will be evident in your performance, and by taking charge of the environment, you will communicate that you are prepared, competent, and worthy of attention.

Using Silence Effectively

The effective use of silence is a powerful communications tool. Unfortunately, most speakers fear silence. Let's say you've just approached a podium to give a speech. If your entrance went smoothly and you sent positive signals with that entrance, you will diminish your effectiveness by starting your speech immediately.

Instead, wait a moment. Take a breath. Relax and take a look around at your audience. *Let some silence happen.* This direction is as applicable to an audience of ten as it is to an audience of two hundred. This bit of silence indicates that you are in charge and you want their attention.

If you ignore this direction and dive right into your remarks, the many conversations that are going on in any audience will be interrupted. At the moment you begin, audience members are more likely to be thinking of their interrupted conversations than of your first words—a poor set of circumstances for even the best of speakers. A few seconds of silence gives them time to shift their attention from their conversations to you. You'll build considerable authority and listenership in that brief moment.

You should also use silence during your speech for emphasis. Before and after a particularly important fact, pause. This works for speeches as well as any of the other communication situations covered in this book. The moment of silence will cause anyone not fully listening to refocus on you and will give greater impact to the phrase punctuated at either end by the silence. In a speech script, you may want to mark your notes to make sure some planned silences occur, especially if you have a habit of speaking rapidly.

In a culture in which talking is success, silence is wrongly viewed as failure. Use this powerful signal behavior to your advantage. With practice, strategically applied, silence can be a real booster of your authority, competence, and self-assurance.

Using Your Eyes to Get Your Message Across

Shakespeare called the eyes "the mirror of the soul." The eyes are a highly important communicator. In this culture, if you don't look at people when you talk to them, it's considered a sign that you might not be telling the truth.

Similarly, if you dart glances around the room while you're speaking, your audience is likely to think you are "shifty" or somehow to be distrusted. Some misguided speakers only look at their notes and attempt to "tune out" the audience. The fact is, the audience just as quickly tunes out such speakers.

The solution to sending the right signals with your eyes is simple and to the point: *look at the person or people you are talking to.* In a courtroom, or in a media or job interview, this means looking at the person who asked the question as you respond.

When you're speaking to a group, the best method of making eye contact varies depending on audience size. You should either look directly at individual audience members as you speak or direct your gaze toward areas of the audience, such as left, center, and right, to give the impression that you are speaking *directly* to each member of the audience. This applies even if the glare of lighting makes your audience invisible from the podium.

I have found that with an audience of about thirty or fewer people, it's possible to make eye contact with each one as I speak. As the audience increases, into the hundreds, directing eye contact toward areas rather than individuals works as well in conveying the impression of eye contact.

At first, maintaining adequate eye contact with your audience requires concentration and practice, as well as familiarity with your notes. After a few successful outings, maintaining eye contact will become a natural part of your delivery.

Remember that the use of your eyes in speaking is one of the chief ways in which you bond with an audience or an individual and give the impression that you are caring, committed, and credible.

A final word of advice on using your eyes to communicate: avoid those ridiculous suggestions we have all heard, such as focusing on and speaking to a distant object in the room or pretending your audience is nude. The first of these silly strategies gives you the blank look of people who've forgotten to take their medication, and the second gives you the silly smile of someone who is overmedicated.

Making Your Point with Gestures

"But what will I do with my hands?" is a question I often hear from those who are about to deliver a major presentation or appear in a media interview. Although I'm not usually fond of answering a question with a question, I ask: "What do you do with them in conversation?"

The fact is that normally we don't pay attention to our hands or our hand gestures. Only the inexperienced speaker in a high-pressure situation tries to examine each and every behavior, including hand gestures, in an effort to assemble the perfect act.

I don't want you to put an act together, but to focus on a few signal behaviors. For example, if you're feeling particularly rigid, you might want to practice a gesture or two—but the best solution is to practice your speech with the thought of including more movement in general, both hand movement and movement around the podium.

It would be easy for me to describe a few key gestures and then tell you to mark your text so as to gesture at certain key points of information. But the result is usually a cue for a hopelessly wooden, staged effect. I once saw a speaker get an unintended laugh (the worst kind) by thrusting two fingers skyward as he said: "And now for my third point . . ."

To get back to my earlier question, "What do you do with your hands in conversation?" the answer is, "Nothing in particular." This should also be your general approach to gestures. They will happen naturally and appropriately if you let them, in conversation or in any other communicative encounter.

You can facilitate your gestures by placing your hands at either corner of the podium, just out of the audience's sight. In an interview, place your hands on your lap, ready to gesture. While either of these positions will make it easy to gesture, folding your arms will make it difficult and will telegraph that you are rigid and uncomfortable, physically, and just maybe psychologically.

Controlling and Managing Your Body Language

The lyric from an old show tune says: "Every little movement has a meaning all its own." Although we don't need to get too theatrical here, where you stand, how you sit, and whether you move around are all manageable signal behaviors that communicate your level of comfort and authority to your audience.

If you're at a podium, decide how you want to manage the space and stick to that plan. You may wish to stay behind the podium during your talk (a wise move if you have a lot of notes) and then move off to one side during the question-and-answer period. Then again, once you have been through a speech a number of times, you may wish to remain in front of the podium, or even do away with it entirely. The important idea here is to decide in *advance*. This way you won't be one of those fidgety, leaning, wandering, or rocking speakers who communicate discomfort and indecisiveness along with their message.

On the matter of posture, the days of standing with hands at sides like some sort of palace centurion are over. You might want to rest your hands on the podium, but be sure to do so gently; don't latch on as if frozen in terror. Try standing in a comfortable position, perhaps with one arm resting on the podium, maybe a hand in a pocket. The point is, you have a stance and posture in which you are most comfortable, and it should be a part of your behavior as you speak.

Body language should communicate comfort, and you can't be comfortable when you focus on a series of planned behaviors. Instead, remember my rule for effective management of body language, which states: *any behavior of body language, posture, or movement that you overuse or constantly repeat becomes distracting to your audience.*

Remember that what you do in a conversation works. Using that behavior as your starting point, make some decision about body language that you're comfortable with. That enhanced level of comfort will be projected to your audience.

Gaining a More Imposing Voice

How do you feel about your speaking voice? Is it too high pitched? Monotonous? Whiny? Most of us are unconcerned with voice until an important speaking occasion pops into our lives; then all the things we don't like about ourselves become ripe for change and adjustment.

Do I Really Sound Like That?

In evaluating the sound of your voice, remember that your speaking voice is very much a function of anatomy: larger people tend to have deeper or lower pitched voices, whereas those of lesser stature and size will often have a higher vocal range. Try to be content with what you have. Even if you're not crazy about the sound of your own voice, if your listeners have no particular reaction, it means they can focus on the message, and that's good for your speech.

Besides, if you somehow change your normal speaking voice (a bad idea) for a presentation or interview, you'll have difficulty keeping up your act, especially when the going gets tough, as in a Q&A period.

If you truly feel you have a problem with voice pitch or quality or a voice that tires or cracks very easily, you might consider seeing a medical specialist or a qualified voice specialist.

But I Sound Monotonous

Fortunately, with practice, monotony is one of the more manageable signal behaviors. Monotonous voices are actually one of two types: the voice that continues at nearly the same pitch or musical note, with very little variation; or the voice that repeats a pattern of pitch and loudness so that every phrase sounds the same.

If you have the typical monotonous voice, it's probably because you are either uncomfortable with the situation or unfamiliar with the material. Your inhibition when it comes to being vocally alive conveys your discomfort to an audience and wrongly signals to them that you are bored, boring, or indifferent.

How to Enhance Your Expressiveness

Here are some steps you can take to enhance vocal expressiveness.

To reduce your level of vocal inhibition, listen to a radio commercial and compare that delivery with your own. You will notice that the commercial has too much variety and expressiveness for conversation; in radio, however, voice is all you have, so announcers tend to be hyperexpressive.

Record your own radio commercial, with the same degree of emphasis as the announcer. Note that I am not referring to the announcer's voice, but to the level of vocal variety that's present in the typical broadcast commercial. Capturing even some of that vocal expressiveness will dramatically increase the level of variety in your normal speaking voice.

Once you can imitate the "announcer" style at will, you should attempt to transfer that degree of vocal variety to the text of a speech you are presenting. In practicing, record portions of your speech with this livelier delivery.

A second technique that's effective for increasing your level of vocal expressiveness is to practice a speech as if you are delivering it to a group of small children. Have you ever noticed how adults talk to young children? Even the most stentorian voice becomes gentle and varied.

No, I'm not suggesting you actually deliver your speech to an audience as if they were a bunch of three-year-olds, but use this exercise to explore and increase your vocal expressiveness. Record your voice and listen to it with a critical ear toward shedding your vocal inhibitions. Practice both these techniques, and once they become internalized, you will find that speaking with increased vocal expressiveness will go from a learned technique to one of your natural signal behaviors.

Maximizing Your Spoken Fluency

Fluency is signal behavior that your audience uses, right or wrong, as a measure of your personal confidence, preparedness, and even competence. We all speak with varying degrees of fluency; some of us fall over words or jumble phrases more often than others. But certain ideas and techniques will help you maximize your spoken fluency.

Remember that *perfect fluency does not happen.* Even conversational speech is actually a series of words punctuated by verbalized pauses (saying "uh" or "you know"), hesitations, and interruptions from other participants in the conversation.

Instead of focusing on trying not to flub (which only makes you nervous and less fluent), become thoroughly familiar with your notes. Read them over repeatedly. I instruct speakers I coach to read through a speech *at least* ten times before attempting to deliver it to an audience. Some speakers are more comfortable with double that amount of run-throughs.

As you read over a speech—practicing aloud is most valuable— mark the places where you tend to stop or trip over a word or phrase. If you have difficulty pronouncing a word, spend some time learning to say the word, or simply go ahead and change it.

Another technique for improving fluency is to make sure you can read your notes. This sounds like an obvious tip until you realize that when you go over your notes, you do so in comfortable surroundings, maybe at your desk or in a favorite chair. Even as you sit in an airliner going over your notes, your eyes are a lot closer to the page than they will be at the podium.

Maintaining eye contact with your audience while keeping your place in hard-to-read notes is virtually impossible. The speaker who attempts to do so usually ends up abandoning the notes altogether, delivering a diluted or disjointed version of the original text.

Avoid this problem with well-marked notes that you can read easily from about three feet. Type them up and print them out in a large, double-spaced font to make them easier to read. This way, you can maintain adequate eye contact and fluency and will communicate a heightened degree of credibility, authority, and impact.

Projecting the Right Visual Image

While it may be socially correct to say that we are generally capable of looking beyond such externals as the appearance of a speaker, there isn't an attorney in the land who would advise his or her client to show up in court wearing bib overalls. Whether you like it or not, especially in important communicative situations, *appearance counts*. Audiences and individuals can and do make judgments based on our appearance.

It's not my purpose to give "dress-for-success" advice, but I would be remiss in not including appearance in any discussion of signal behaviors. I'll leave the specifics of apparel choice to your own fashion sense and to the experts in that field, but I would advise you to be attentive to two areas: (1) audience expectations and (2) minimalization of distraction.

Be Who They Expect

Examine your role in communicating with an audience. As a senior executive, witness, candidate, or spokesperson dealing with a sensitive issue, your personal credibility and the level of personal stability you communicate become especially crucial.

Just as you're unlikely to see an airline captain in a clown suit (and might get off the plane if you did), those with whom you will be speaking have certain expectations—not only about what you will say but also about how you will look. Think about those expectations and attempt to meet them. In doing so, you will make those listeners comfortable enough to focus on your message more than on your appearance.

Minimize Distractions

As soon as I mention meeting audience expectations concerning appearance, the more contrarian reader (or anyone whose top-ten songs include "I've Got to Be Me") will think things such as, *I've got to make a fashion statement to get their attention.* Perhaps you even have a fashion trademark, maybe a hat or a crossword-puzzle tie.

Truly effective communication enables an audience to focus on the message, which, if you are to make the sale or convince the jury or achieve any other purpose, is best accomplished in an atmosphere free of distractions. Let your message be the focal point of your communicative effort, not your attire.

Showing Your Qualifications

The failure to establish your credentials is a missed opportunity to establish your credibility.

The media are loaded with such characters as TV weather forecasters who are not meteorologists, mail-order marketers masquerading as experts, and even people who give medical advice or sell health products after delivering such incredibly absurd disclaimers as, "I'm not a doctor, but I play one on TV . . ."

Credentials are conveniently ignored by those who don't have them, and, in what seems like some sort of false modesty, those of us with significant experience or specialized knowledge of an issue tend not to talk about it. My advice? Never talk to an audience or participate in any serious communicative event, from the media interview to the witness stand, without mentioning your qualifications.

As a speaker who is particularly qualified to be expressing an opinion or position on an issue, you give greater weight to your remarks and boost your credibility by telling your audience just what it is that qualifies you. Failure to do so raises doubts in the minds of your more critical or astute listeners. So tell them, as soon as possible, what your credentials are.

Credentials don't have to consist of a string of academic degrees. You might have served for an impressive number of years in your field—an equivalent to a diploma in most listeners' minds. If you're short on time in an industry, perhaps you have some special training or have thoroughly researched the issue on your own.

The point is to say something on the credentials issue. Most speakers don't. If you do, especially in a debate or panel discussion, you establish your personal credibility and authority and increase the impact of your message.

Reducing Your Anxiety Level

Note that I have not said *don't be anxious*. Nor am I about to present a magic formula for ridding yourself of speaker anxiety because, short of medication (which I don't advise), it doesn't exist.

If you are a victim of stage fright or speaker anxiety, it helps to understand why you feel this way. Many of the speakers I work with have lengthy explanations containing gobs of psycho-babble to explain their anxiety. They're probably anxious, however, because they are ill-prepared or overtired, or else they've failed to implement many of the techniques outlined in this chapter.

My point is that you shouldn't become overly focused on speaker anxiety. Sure you're under pressure, and yes, everyone will be looking at you, but, beyond that, audiences are usually sympathetic and supportive, particularly with the less experienced speaker. Keep your anxiety level in perspective. At this point, overdiscussing or analyzing speaker anxiety will only heighten it.

Summary

We have been discussing various signal behaviors and tactics to help you enhance your communicative performance. Review these tactics and behaviors and focus on a few that may detract from your effectiveness as a speaker. *How* you deliver your message, rather than *what* you actually say, can greatly alter an audience's perception of how competent, authoritative, and credible you are.

If you are planning on a major overhaul of your spoken delivery skills, do so a few steps at a time. The key to success here is to put together a series of signal behaviors that send positive messages about you and your ability, rather than "an act" that will come apart as soon as you encounter a stressful situation.

If you adjust your communicative behavior gradually, you can remain comfortable and behaviorally consistent, whether the climate is friendly or hostile. It is this level of comfort and consistency that will send positive signals about you and your message to an audience, making you the most powerful communicator you can be.

Quick Review:
Nonverbal Communications Skills

1. Check out the presentation site in advance. Familiarity breeds comfort.

2. Pause at the beginning of a speech; let your audience settle down.

3. Eye contact is important. Look directly at your audience, whether it's of one or many.

4. Don't use staged gestures; they look phony. Instead, relax and let them happen.

5. Avoid being rigid about posture. Stand or sit comfortably.

6. Practice maintaining vocal expressiveness; otherwise, don't try to change your voice, based on some ill-defined ideal.

7. Don't focus on fluency. Know your notes, have a text you can read easily, and remember that perfect fluency is an unrealistic goal.

8. Regarding your personal appearance, be comfortable but be what the audience expects.

9. Tell an audience—any audience—your credentials and your qualifications for being there.

10. Work on a few signal behaviors at a time, blending them into your spoken delivery, rather than putting together an act.

CHAPTER TWO

Improving Your Language Power

AT-A-GLANCE SUMMARY

This chapter helps you to increase the impact of your spoken words. The more vivid your message, the greater its impact and memorability.

Although the emphasis is on the speaker's podium, this information applies to every situation, from media interviews to sales presentations.

You Are What You Say

An old commercial selling "vocabulary-building" tapes proclaims: "People can tell a lot about you from the words you use." I don't know how effective the tapes were, but I do agree that your listeners make judgments based on your language choices, whether in a speech, in a sales presentation, or even in your testimony in court.

Listeners make judgments about such vital areas as your level of knowledge, experience, and education; whether you are open and forthcoming or seem to have something to hide; or even whether you can be trusted and believed. Whether audience members are dressed in three-piece suits or bib overalls, they can tell when something about your message bothers them or doesn't quite ring true.

The same audience may be bored by your speech, or they may find your message highly listenable and memorable, based on your choice of language.

Despite the existence of such devices as vocabulary tapes, there is no magical word list to guarantee results each time you talk. If there were a list of power words, so many speakers would use all the power words so often that, much like the overexposed celebrity, they would soon lose any power they had in the first place.

Effective use of language means using your own personal style of conversing with an audience while adapting to that audience's frame of reference. Effective language needs to be genuinely yours, not borrowed like rented formal wear. Effective language also means being as understandable as possible without being patronizing.

While maintaining your own personal style is an important element in helping you use language, building on that style will help you increase your effectiveness by increasing the listenability and memorability of your remarks.

Using Conversational Language to Increase Your Power

At any black-tie or formal dinner, you can usually spot the guys in the rented tuxedos. They look just a bit stiff and wooden. The garment doesn't quite fit the way it should; it's a little bit off. But as the wearer will readily tell you, it's just a rental.

When you deliver a speech and use language you have borrowed just for the occasion—the words are someone else's or the speech contains words you wouldn't normally use—you come off like the gentleman in the rented tux: a bit stiff, uncomfortable, and generally feeling out of your element.

Whether the speech is your own or your remarks have been written for you, as is often the case in the corporate sphere, go over your notes and delete or change phrases that sound the least bit alien to you. A good speechwriter will observe your personal style and quickly become capable of writing to match it.

Your specific speaking style, just like your personality, will be influenced by your environment and experience. Such factors as your occupation, how well read you are, your educational background, and whether you are a creature of the sciences or the arts are all factors that influence your linguistic choices and how you come across to an audience.

Many of those who write on language usage will stress the importance of being conversational with your audiences, and I agree with that advice. But don't do so at the expense of your usual vocabulary. If you do so, you'll be talking down to your audience, and they'll know it.

Select the Most Effective Words

I once knew a prominent college professor who seemed almost intimidated by his own stature. One reflection of his discomfort was that he spoke in language that no one else, even professors, would ever use. Instead of saying that the faculty should pay more attention to something, he made statements such as, "The faculty should lend greater consequence to the issue of . . ."

I've long since forgotten the issues of which that professor spoke, but I do remember that his language choices were a linguistic gymnastics exhibition. Most of his colleagues paid more attention to *how* rather than *what* he said.

Once language becomes a performance activity, a means to dazzle rather than communicate, the all-important message itself becomes obscured.

Following are some examples of words and phrases that are more conversational and effective than their perfectly acceptable but less memorable counterparts. In categorizing some words and phrases as "nonconversational," I don't mean to suggest that they are not useful, but that their infrequent use in spoken language makes them unusual to the listener and therefore more likely to divert attention from your message.

Here is a list of language choices I would make in writing a speech, the conversational words being the preferred choices:

NONCONVERSATIONAL	CONVERSATIONAL
connotes	also means
de jure	according to law
erudite	studious, learned
eviscerate	weaken
fallacious	false, misleading

NONCONVERSATIONAL	CONVERSATIONAL
forlorn	sad, miserable
faux	imitation
largesse	generosity
libation	drink
invidious	offensive, malicious
invective	insults
macro-	very large
micro-	very small
maudlin	overly sentimental
melancholia	depression
myriad	great number
obstinate	stubborn
onerous	troublesome
oxymoronic	contradictory
penurious	stingy
pedestrian	ordinary
perspicacious	wise, discerning
petulant	irritable
redouble	intensify, double
render	cause
rout	defeat
salacious	obscene
schema, scheme	plan
sensorial	sensory
sonorous	rich-sounding
torpor	sluggishness
unctuous	falsely earnest, oily
vex	annoy
wallow	roll around, luxuriate
warrant	justify, authorize

Most of us don't use words in the left column in conversation, yet you might be tempted to use them in a speech to make things more formal or to impress your audience. *Don't do it.* Trying to boost your linguistic octane rating with words you normally don't use merely makes you uncomfortable and increases the psychological distance between you and your audience.

An important difference between written and spoken language is that the reader can slow down or even come to a dead halt in the middle of a page in order to figure out the author's exact meaning. In spoken language, however, if your listener takes a mental break to ponder an obscure word, part of the message will be lost, since you're still talking.

The key is to use the level of vocabulary that makes you comfortable and that your audience understands fully. If your vocabulary is more wide-ranging than most, remember that such a vocabulary means more than knowing a lot of big words. It also means you have more options—you can make word choices that will maximize your audience's ability to understand and retain your message.

Avoiding the Definition Trap:
Know Exactly What You Mean

Once, an undergraduate student of mine who probably didn't have time to write a speech introduction came up against one of these corollaries of education that most veteran students already know: your chances of being called on are inversely proportional to your degree of preparedness.

She "borrowed" some words from a magazine article to begin her speech, words that went something like: "The deep purple of the predawn darkness was relinquishing its grasp on a sky that yearned to take on a more azure hue, almost as if to be in greater harmony with the burgeoning bustle of the awakening metropolis."

This description of an urban dawn was considerably more elaborate than most undergraduate students will venture for a minor assignment in a basic speech course. I suspected that she had little to do with the authorship of her opening words. Exposing this bit of chicanery consisted of no more than my asking the student exactly what the word "azure" meant. Of course, she had no idea, thereby learning hard and fast what Abraham Lincoln said about not being able to fool people.

The fact is, speakers often use words they don't fully understand. Some think no one will notice; others think they know the meaning of a word but have it wrong. Don't fall into the trap of faking it. If a speech is written for you, and you are not familiar with each and every word—not only in the context of the speech, but in general— look it up.

Even if it's a basic or generic term, be prepared to define it. This point was very well made to me by a longtime employee of an electric company, who, after having made dozens of successful safety presentations to groups of school children, was badly stumped by the horribly obvious question that could only come from the uncluttered mind of a child: "What's electricity?"

My friend uttered one of those embarrassing but momentarily useful things we say when completely stuck, such as: "Well, everybody knows that . . . and it's right there in the outlet for all of us to use." Of course, he went straight home, looked up the answer, and is now a master of knowing the *exact* meaning of his remarks.

The same principle, knowing the exact meaning of what you are saying, also applies in scientific and technical circles. Often, a common term will be contained in a report, or an abbreviation will be used so frequently that everyone assumes everyone else will know what it means.

I once asked a corporate spokesperson who was talking about PCB disposal what "PCB" stood for. Although he had been dealing with the issue for some time, he had no idea it stood for "polychlorinated biphenyl." He was relieved that the question had come up in a training session and not in front of an audience.

When writing a speech or presentation, make certain that you know the meanings of any terms you'll be using and don't overlook terms or abbreviations you've used for years, the ones "everybody knows."

Managing Abbreviations and Technical Language

Have you ever noticed that pilots and nurses talk in initials? Airplane talk is filled with such gems as the ILS, RVR, AGL, ETA, FL, and TCA.

Nurses are those people you meet in the ER who take your BP, set up an EKG, and even administer CPR before sending you to the ICU. Once these people stop using initials and start using words, you almost wish they'd lose the jargon and go back to abbreviations; at least the initials took less time.

No matter what your chosen field, technical jargon and abbreviations have probably become a part of your vocabulary. Remember that you are shutting some of your audience out by using abbreviations or jargon. Even if they figure out what you are saying by the end of your presentation, they have not heard your entire message.

If you ignore your audience's level of knowledge and indiscriminately dump abbreviations and jargon into your speech, you will come across as smug, uncaring, and inconsiderate, or ignorant of your audience's range of familiarity with your topic.

The solution? If you know that some audience members will have familiarity with your topic and others will have none, you might begin by saying something like, "I know that some of you here are old pros in the insurance game, but others of you haven't heard me talk on this subject before. Therefore, if you pros will bear with me, I'll let the rest of you know just what all those abbreviations mean as I get to them in this presentation."

If your speech is going to contain a large number of important abbreviations and you see that your audience contains a large number of neophytes, you might do the "old-pro" disclaimer and take your audience through some of the abbreviations before beginning your prepared speech. The point here is to let the audience know that you're open, communicative, and considerate and that you want to communicate your ideas clearly and effectively to *everyone* present. The "old pros" will appreciate the fact that you have acknowledged their presence, and the new people will feel welcome and included. All will do a better job of listening.

Name Names and Speak in the First Person

Sometimes a spoken message suffers because of what you leave out rather than what you include.

Recently, in helping a senior executive prepare for a major speech, we reviewed a tape of an earlier speech in which it was his task to detail some of the serious problems his company was having. I pointed out that at no time, in a speech that lasted nearly thirty minutes, did he mention the name of the company—odd behavior for a senior executive, and not exactly a display of corporate pride.

His reaction to this lapse was initially one of disbelief. Upon reviewing the tape, however, he agreed that he had tried not to associate the company name with the problems he was detailing. Nice try, but I doubt his ploy fooled the audience.

When you make such linguistic decisions in an attempt to shift or deemphasize blame, all you communicate is your own discomfort, usually calling more attention to the very problem you were trying to minimize.

Have you ever heard a child tell his or her parents about grades? Inevitably the conversation goes something like: "I got an A in Spanish, a B in chemistry, and *he gave me* a C in history." Our little student's intention is to take credit for everything positive ("I got . . .") and assign blame for anything negative ("he gave me . . .").

Similarly, when things are going well, the typical corporate spokesperson's presentation is full of pronouns and references to the company: "I'm very proud, in fact all of us at American Plexon Corporation are proud to announce that the groundbreaking ceremonies for our new design center will take place on . . ." Yet when there are problems, that same spokesperson makes the same kind of linguistic shift as did our school kid. The American Plexon spokesperson, on a topic much less pleasant than the new design center, is more likely to say: "The company has determined that the spill has been contained and that efforts are already under way to minimize the environmental impact."

American Plexon becomes "the company," and pronouns and specific references to the employees disappear. Notice that "efforts are under way" is a highly impersonal way of saying that the company is doing something.

While this statement gets the facts across, it also implies, by what it doesn't say, that serious problems must be present, as signified by the lack of any reassurance.

The listener's conclusion? Something is up—if not something serious, at least something American Plexon would rather not talk about.

In contrast, the same statement delivered in a more personal style, with a more reassuring tone, can sound like this: "American Plexon has sent a team to examine the spill at our plant, and our personnel want me to reassure you that the job of minimizing the impact has already been started by our environmental safety crews."

The tone in the second statement suggests that while there is a problem, company personnel are taking care of it and that those people care enough to want to communicate the situation. In this statement, American Plexon comes across as an organization with the integrity to tell the consumer, stockholder, reporter, or whoever that audience may be exactly what is going on and what is being done about it—a tremendous improvement over the responsibility-shifting "He gave me a C" approach of the earlier statement.

Speaking in Color, not in Black and White

The most memorable or colorful speakers are invariably those who provide descriptions in the form of images and analogies that their audiences remember.

Colorful analogies and descriptions come from a wide variety of sources, and as a speaker you'll need to be on the lookout for them. I once read a description of an automobile's cluttered dashboard as a "Tokyo by night instrument panel." W.C. Fields, in one of his films, described a gaudily arrayed old woman as being "all dressed up like a well-kept grave."

References to sports, pop culture, or world events also help add that quality of color to language while they show that you have the imagination and the vision to look beyond the scope of your own field for inspiration and ideas.

Of course, your analogies and descriptions should fit your audience. Describing a failure as a "fallen soufflé" at a sports dinner is as bad as describing a success as a "triple-crown winner" to a gathering of gourmands. Similarly the demographic profile of your audience is going to shape the definition of what is colorful and popular and what isn't.

If you don't reach into literature, the arts, sports, or the less-traveled corners of your own mind for imaginative descriptors of the events and situations you present, then the audience will describe you much the way a colleague of mine described a particularly dull job candidate after an interview: "He had a gray suit, gray hair, and gray tie . . . and a gray face."

Beware of the "Peter Piper Picked a Peck" Syndrome

One of my major objectives in helping you succeed as a communicator is getting you to be comfortable at the speaker's podium. You have learned a series of behaviors to make yourself comfortable, such as taking the time to arrange your notes, not beginning right away, even having a sip or two of water—all ways of relaxing as you begin your speech.

In the same connection, the language contained in your speech shouldn't make you uneasy. Yet, just as I am convinced that the preparers of some exotic cuisines spice their food just to see how much diners can endure, I think linguists have devised words that should never be spoken aloud, not because they are obscene or offensive, but simply because they are unpronounceable or make speakers stumble.

Among the worst offenders in the category of unpronounceable words are such monsters as "homogeneity," "homonymous," "magnanimity," "specificity," "inestimable," "serendipitous," and "statistics" or "statistical." You can probably add to this list with a selection of your own.

There are other words that speakers tend to trip over because they are unfamiliar with them. Among those I've noticed over the years are "nuclear," "et cetera," "epitome," "auxiliary," "concomitant," "subsidiary," "prescient," and "synergistic."

A good rule to follow is that *if you are rehearsing a speech aloud (which you should) and you stumble over a word more than once, change it to a more easily pronounced word or phrase.*

The alternative is to circle it and repeat the problem phrase over and over; unfortunately, this usually doesn't work. Once at the lectern, you'll most likely flub the word or phrase, although you'll see it coming, since you've marked your notes. Having built-in flub points only adds to your discomfort.

Of course, there are times when you just can't change the language. (I once gave a talk on a visual problem called homonymous hemianopsia.) Then the rule is one of rehearse, rehearse, rehearse. With practice, the most difficult pronunciations can be made dramatically easier.

Remember, a nearly impossible phrase such as, "Let's examine the specific statistics in our study that show . . ." can just as easily be communicated with the words, "Let's take a look at the exact numbers in our study that show . . ." Leave Peter Piper and his pickled peppers to the first graders.

Keeping Your Audience's Attention

Studies have shown that audiences tend to listen to very little of what you say, not out of malice or boredom, but because they can listen—and think—a lot more quickly than you can talk. Once a listener figures out where you are going, he or she will switch to thinking about such weighty matters as whether the dog has been fed, or the car is locked, or what time the bank closes and whether you'll finish talking by then.

There are several ways to deal with the sporadic nature of listening and get the audience back on your frequency, especially when you are about to cover an important piece of information or to present a crucial argument.

The Power of "Command Phrases"

Sometimes you give a speech intended to encourage your audience to take action or adopt your point of view. Command phrases are those that directly demand action. Attention phrases are those that could be delivered by a commander or a coach to gain that extra effort from those in his or her charge.

If your speech has this kind of purpose, check it for command phrases that will increase the impact of your remarks and impress your audience with the need for action. Here are some command phrases that will recapture a listener's wandering attention:

- "It's essential that you remember . . ."
- "If you leave here with only one thought . . ."
- "Here is the answer you all want to know . . ."
- "Let me repeat that . . ."
- "It's absolutely critical to understand that . . ."
- "Even if you disagree, you'll find that . . ."
- "Listen to this . . ."
- "The fact is this . . ."
- "Regardless of what you've heard before . . ."

- "It all boils down to one important piece of evidence . . ."
- "The unavoidable conclusion is this . . ."

Command phrases tell an audience to "listen up," since what is to follow is especially important.

Use Ordinal Phrases

Although less dramatic than some of the other language tactics I have been talking about, ordinal phrases serve as important markers in bracketing and organizing various parts of your speech.

They tell an audience that one area of information has concluded and the next is about to begin, and they give your audience a sense of where you are in the speech. They make it easy for the listener to join you "in progress" and to pick up on the essential parts of your message. This is important, since all listeners, despite your best efforts, tend to tune in and out during a speech. Here are some useful ordinal phrases:

- "First of all . . ."
- "Secondly . . ."
- "The next area to consider is the fact that . . ."
- "Another important factor . . ."
- "In this final portion of my remarks . . ."
- "Finally . . ."
- "Last but not least . . ."
- "Let me leave with one final thought . . ."

Check your speech for various types of command and ordinal phrases. A speech presentation missing these elements of language lacks emphasis and clarity.

Effective use of these devices will not only improve an audience member's ability to listen to your message but will also give you greater control over which parts of the message your audience will remember most. This is an especially important feature in a speech such as a sales presentation or any message seeking a specific outcome.

Mention Audience Members by Name

Another way to increase listenership and retention of your message is to refer to audience members by name. "As both Alice in engineering and Jared in finance will tell you . . ." is a sure way not only to get Alice's and Jared's attention but also to raise the possibility that you may be making specific reference to others present.

Perhaps the tension you create in the audience is a vestige of the terror we all felt in elementary school when we didn't have the homework and the teacher started calling names—but it works.

While I'm on the subject of naming names, the preceding technique should not be confused with the annoying habit some speakers have of constantly referring to or delivering asides to an audience member that most of those present do not know. While such references suggest a bond between you and that person, they can also create a rift between you and the rest of the audience, an inference that the audience member is privy to some exclusive information or a feeling that you'd rather be chatting with your colleague than giving a speech.

Make Your Talk Audience-Specific

Even if you don't make specific reference to members of your audience, you should still refer directly to your audience, to remove any "generic" tone the speech may have. Always mention the name of the organization, not only just as you begin, but also in the text of your speech, especially before your most important points. Phrases such as "each of you" or "every one of us here today" give the talk a more personal tone, as if you were talking as much to individuals as you were to a large group.

Make Numbers Visible

If you say to an audience that twenty million people suffer from alcoholism or some other form of addictive behavior, the reaction is likely to be somewhere between "that's mildly interesting" and "so what." If you say, however, "Figures point to the fact that two of the twenty people here today will be afflicted by addictive behavior at some point in their lives," the reaction is likely to be a lot more personal and the impact much greater.

The problem with big numbers, especially those up there in the millions, is that we can't visualize them. Thus they have little or no impact on us. The solution is to reduce the number to smaller quantities, as in the preceding paragraph, or to paint a word picture of just how big a number you are talking about.

A good example of such a word picture was expressed by the late mathematician Edward Kasner in explaining the size of a number called a googol (one followed by one hundred zeros, from which we get "Google," in a play on the company's mission to organize the seemingly endless information on the Web). Dr. Kasner explained that the number of raindrops falling on Manhattan in a century is much less than a googol.

Politicians have had considerable difficulty in expressing the seriousness of the massive national debt. From another perspective, politicians have had little difficulty in letting that debt soar, in part because numbers in trillions represent unfathomable quantities. Perhaps this is why you won't hear many of those same politicians increase the impact of that number by stating it as "$60,000 for each man, woman, and child," or "a debt that is growing at $13,000 per second."

Whether you are talking about sales figures, the life cycle of a product, or any set of numbers of such size as to make your listener's eyes glaze over, get out your calculator and reduce those numbers to a manageable level. Your audience will appreciate it and will remember the facts.

What's Your Motivation?

Usually asked of actors to help them develop and intensify a character, "What's your motivation?" is a question you should ask yourself as you review the text of any speech you are about to give.

More specifically, what is the emotional tone or mood you wish to establish in your audience with your remarks? Are you proud of an accomplishment, and do you want to instill a sense of pride in your audience? Is there a sense of urgency or crisis that must be impressed on your audience in order to move them to action?

Establishing an Emotional Tone to Move Your Audience

Unity, anger, pride, commitment, joy, and even feelings of peace are all possible emotional responses to the language you use. If you are proud, excited, delighted, or outraged, have you told your audience in just those words? If you want your audience to share in or adopt those feelings as their own, have you said so, again in those specific terms? I call these phrases and words *E-words*.

Speakers who aren't at the podium regularly will often comment to me that they worry about boring their audiences. Using more E-words will energize any presentation. Increasing the emotionality of your talk need not mean that you jump around the stage or rant like a top-forty disc jockey announcing this week's big hit.

It is true that your vocal and physical animation can enhance the perceived level of emotionality, but gaining the kind of emotional response you want from an audience begins with your choice of language.

The following E-word list not only illustrates this point, but should also be helpful in determining whether the emotionality of the language in your speech is compatible with your motivation or the emotional intent you wish to communicate.

E-LEVEL CHART

LOW-TO-NO E-LEVEL	HIGH E-LEVEL
I'm here to talk about . . .	I'm happy to be here . . .
You have accomplished a lot.	I hope you're proud that . . .
There's much good news.	Let me tell you the most sensational news!
This is an important time.	During this truly great moment . . .
We should all be concerned . . .	Let me assure you, I share your anger at . . .
We are faced with a serious situation.	Make no mistake—this is a crisis.
Your immediate involvement . . .	Each of us must act now.
This isn't fair.	This is a gross injustice.
It's imperative that we act.	We can and must take action.
The decision is yours.	Here is what each of you must do.

In each case, the high E-level phrases make use of words that will evoke a greater emotional response from your audience, that is, a sense of crisis, gross injustice, anger, joy, or festivity. Also note the use of the imperative ("must") and superlative ("most sensational") whenever possible and appropriate.

Increasing the use of such E-level phrases and referring specifically to your audience ("each and every one here" instead of the simple plural pronoun "you") are techniques that should be combined to intensify the impact of your message, which will be more personal and will have the desired emotional effect on your audience.

Repeat Key Phrases

"That's important; let me repeat that."

Another simple yet effective technique for giving greater emphasis to certain portions of your remarks is to repeat key phrases or important facts or figures. If your speech contains a lot of numbers, pause before saying them and repeat those that are crucial in getting your message across. Such repetition for emphasis will sound this way: "In spite of increased sales figures, we are still three million dollars behind last year . . . three million dollars."

Watch Your Pronouns

English is a real *man's* language. (Feminists will please note the intended irony here.) One of the most offensive speeches I ever heard was given by the dean of a business college at commencement. I say offensive because, as the dean rambled on about the great sacrifices made by the men in the graduating class, I looked around and noticed that about a third of the class were women.

The problem is that we have a sexist language that most heavily favors the male side of things. Going along with the crowd, linguistically speaking, will not only be offensive to the more astute members of the audience but may also be so distracting that your original message will be obscured. I've often heard sentences such as: "If we get the opinion of the best attorney we can find, here is what *he* will say," thereby excluding women from the ranks of those best attorneys.

The solution? Watch your pronouns. You will note that this book, wherever appropriate, includes the male and female pronouns. If you have the need to refer to a best attorney or surgeon or any profession or trade, I'd recommend the "he and she" form when your reference requires pronouns. The more socially aware members of any audience will take notice of such inclusion and appreciate the consideration. Male and female pronouns should be used, not as part of a crusade in the name of political correctness, but because no audience can fully listen to a message that in some way offends them.

Keep your audience focused on the message by making certain that your pronouns and your occupational examples are free of sexist references and include women, rather than excluding them, as the language so often does in its usual state.

Summary

I agree with that radio commercial I mentioned at the beginning of this chapter: people do judge you by the words you use. Don't put on an act. Keep your language conversational; build emphasis and increase impact with some of the tactics outlined in this chapter. If you do so, your audience will be able to focus on your message and retain it.

Quick Review:
Improving Your Language Power

1. Keep your language conversational; simpler is better.

2. Know the exact meaning and pronunciation of every word you use. (If you're not sure, look it up!)

3. Don't keep your company or product name a secret.

4. Explain every abbreviation or acronym at least once, especially the first time you use it.

5. Use examples and images to which your audience can relate.

6. Make sure your language choices convey the right emotion (pride, anger, joy, commitment) to your audience.

7. Use ordinal-phrase language to tell us where you are in a speech (*first of all, second, finally,* and so on).

8. Always make at least one specific mention of your audience in any speech.

9. Boil numbers down to quantities that people can envision.

10. It's a sexist language. Watch your pronouns.

CHAPTER THREE

Becoming a Better Listener

This chapter is about making you a better listener. Much miscommunication and misunderstanding happen because the listening side of the communication equation is ignored, as it usually is.

This chapter includes tactics for improving your ability to ask the right questions, managing perceptive barriers that impede listening, and taking effective notes.

During the early years of the *Saturday Night Live* telecasts, the late Gilda Radner portrayed a delightfully funny character by the name of Emily Litella. Emily would deliver indignant tirades on such subjects as "burp control" or "moron poverty," only to be reminded that she was supposed to be speaking on birth control or the war on poverty. Once made aware of her error, she ended her tirades abruptly with an embarrassed gaze and an apologetic, "Never mind!"

Emily was funny because she never quite got the message right, even though she expended tremendous energy and passion expressing her concerns. Emily either couldn't hear or just didn't listen, resulting in wasted energy and lots of laughs. Many of us suffer such lapses in listening; while they may not be the stuff of comedy skits, they can be a serious barrier to effective communication.

Poor listening can result in costly mistakes on the witness stand, in the media interview, or in any other communicative encounter. On the other hand, effective listening can give you a distinct advantage as you react to a questioner, listen to a sales presentation, or when exact recall is in your best interests.

Learning to listen effectively and clearly is an often overlooked way to improve your communication skills.

Listening, the act of hearing, perceiving, and retaining spoken information is by nature an inefficient process. A classic study in listening behavior by Paul Rankin found that we spend nearly half (42 percent) of the business day's communicative activity listening.[1] Other studies of our listening behavior further indicate that within eight hours we forget one-third to one-half of what we've heard.

Identifying Barriers to Effective Listening

Thinking Too Quickly

The fact is that no one listens all the time. Rather, we engage in a kind of selective listening known to communications theorists as "out-listening." We begin by listening to a speaker; then, as soon as we figure out what he or she is probably going to say, we tune out and think about something else until we hear a word or phrase that gets our attention once more. This process is repeated over and over again in most listening situations.

You have experienced out-listening if you have ever sat in a meeting, listened to the speaker for a short time, realized you already saw a memo on the subject, and immediately went to wondering if you brought your dry cleaning tickets today. The major problem with out-listening is that it leaves you not with a memory of what the speaker actually said, but with a memory of what you *think* he or she probably said.

Can you avoid out-listening? Not entirely, because we think faster than we speak. Most of us talk at somewhere between 120 and 150 words per minute in most situations. Studies indicate, however, that a

---

1. Paul T. Rankin, "Measurement of the Ability to Understand Spoken Language," unpublished doctoral dissertation (Ann Arbor: University of Michigan, 1926), reported in R. Adler and G. Rodman, *Understanding Human Communication* (New York: Holt, Rinehart & Winston, 1985), 74.

person can process information at anywhere from 500 to 800 words per minute, depending on the subject and the individual. This disparity between rate of speech and your ability to figure out where the speaker is going is one reason your attention tends to wander.

How Expectations and Perceptions Affect Listening

Another barrier to effective listening is that our expectations shape what we hear. In a song called "The Boxer," Simon and Garfunkel sing, "A man hears what he wants to hear and disregards the rest." The lyric is a good synopsis of how selective we can be when it comes to listening. If we arrive at a meeting expecting to hear bad news, we are more likely to retain that part of the message than other portions that may mitigate the negative aspects.

Perception, or your way of looking at an idea or issue, also shapes how well and how much of the message you will receive and retain. We all listen to the spoken message with a set of experiences and knowledge, through which we filter what we hear. This is part of the reason that fifty people, if asked to write a synopsis of a speech they have just heard, will produce fifty different, and sometimes widely varying, messages.

Avoid Becoming a "Pseudo-Listener"

Sometimes fatigue, or the wish to be somewhere else, can result in pretend or pseudo-listening. As the pseudo-listener, you will look attentive, nod in agreement at appropriate times, and even ask a question at the end of a presentation just to prove you were listening; you actually tuned out the entire presentation and were deep in thought about something else.

Another kind of pseudo-listening involves a kind of refined out-listening, so that if the speaker challenges the pseudo-listener with a statement such as, "You haven't heard a word I've said," the pseudo-listener can parrot back anywhere from the last sentence to the last paragraph.

The difference between real listening and this brand of pseudo-listening is that the pseudo-listener retains little or nothing of what was said, listening only in case there is the need to parrot back any of the information covered, information that will be forgotten immediately after the meeting ends.

Overcoming the Obstacle of Challenge-Listening

Another flawed form of listening many of us engage in is what I call challenge-listening. Whereas most audience members are there to hear a message, as the challenge-listener, you are there to have an argument based on your expectation of what the speaker will say. This kind of prejudicially based listening means that you will wait for the speaker to make what you consider an error in content or logic or to use a term that is difficult if not impossible to define.

Once you have found the flaw, there is little reason to listen further; as the typical challenge-listener, you either cease listening altogether and sharpen your fangs for the upcoming question-and-answer period, or listen only for further "evidence" to bolster the argument you now anticipate with such glee. If you engage in challenge-listening, you will not listen to the entire message, only pieces.

If you need to refute the speaker's remarks, you won't be able to do a good job. This is because the challenge-listener's arguments are often one-dimensional and flimsy since they are based on a partial reception of the message.

Instead, try what I call "acceptance-listening." This means that when you anticipate disagreeing with a speaker, make a conscious decision not to agree with but to "accept" his or her entire statement without engaging in silent rebuttal like a challenge-listener.

Challenge-listening can be seen in what passes for political debates in this culture. Typically, candidates avoid listening to and responding to the substance of each other's remarks in favor of waiting for the opponent to utter a phrase that will trigger a planned response—in the hope of gaining the most media attention and thereby becoming the perceived victor.

Senator Lloyd Bentsen's now famous debate rejoinder to then vice-presidential candidate Dan Quayle, "You're no Jack Kennedy...," is a good example of challenge-listening tactics. We all remember the remark, but few if any remember the context of the remark, because it was intended as a personal attack rather than an attempt to deal with a broader issue.

If your focus becomes so narrow that you wait for the slightest misstatement or indefinable term, you may very well miss the point of the message and even the opportunity to engage in a more substantial rebuttal.

Managing Your "Automatic Shutoff"

Have you ever avoided a meeting because a quick look at the agenda brought you to the rapid conclusion that it would be a waste of your time? Sometimes you will sit through a speaker's presentation thinking the same thing, but because leaving would cause too big a disruption or be noticed by too many of your peers, you decide instead to take mental rather than physical leave. In other words, you employ a mode of nonlistening I call "automatic shutoff."

If you add this behavior to the degree of out-listening you normally do in any setting, be assured that you will retain virtually nothing of what is being said. Automatic shutoff behavior can take place not only because you find the topic unpalatable; perhaps it's the wrong time of day or you have a plane to catch or it's your fifth meeting of the day.

Whatever the reason, engaging the automatic shutoff means that you'll miss out on virtually the entire message, even if it contains some interesting or important ideas.

How to Avoid Being Distracted

Sometimes you will be distracted by the speaker to the extent that you find focusing on the message difficult. You may remember that in school, if a teacher had a mannerism, students would make a point of counting how many times that mannerism occurred rather than focusing on the lesson being taught. (My high school algebra teacher once said the word "particularly" forty-five times in one hour.) The poor listening habits I employed at that time enabled me to remember that extraordinarily useless piece of information while retaining little of the mathematical information covered.

Focusing on the style of the speaker impedes your ability to listen. When you focus on the presentation (the language used, the appropriateness of the topic, the length of the message, the speaker's appearance, voice, or nonverbal behavior), you are taking valuable attention away from the message itself.

As you listen, you may conclude that the speaker is selling sizzle rather than steak or that the message contains little of substance—but you can't even make that decision unless you focus on the message itself rather than the stylistic elements that accompany it.

Control Your Listening Environment

Eliminate or minimize environmental distractions. If there is too much noise or visual distraction for you to listen effectively, politely suggest that the meeting be moved or the noise be stopped. If you, as a motivated listener, are having difficulty listening, so will anyone else present and there is little point in continuing.

Remember that noise can be visual as well as auditory. For example, if you are listening to a speaker in a hotel ballroom while in the background a work crew is quietly filling a net with balloons and hoisting them to the ceiling for a later celebration, you and other members of the audience are more likely to be captivated by this visually interesting activity than by the innards of the quarterly financial report.

Have the distraction stopped. Always attend to the environment so you can focus on the message, even if it requires a momentary disruption of the proceedings. Maybe the speaker will have read my words on handling distractions, and you won't have to take action.

Get a Good Seat

If you're listening to a presentation in a room with a hundred other people and you're sitting in the back row, you've severely limited your ability to listen effectively by increasing your physical distance from the speaker.

Whenever anyone receives notice of a phone message, you'll know about it. If people leave early or arrive late, you'll see it and perhaps want to speculate on their comings and goings. If someone drops his or her notes or falls asleep, or if coffee or refreshments are being delivered, you'll be more aware of it than anyone in the room—all because you're sitting in the back.

If listening is important, sit as close to the front as you can. In so doing, not only do you reduce the distance between you and the speaker, you also eliminate most if not all of the distractions referred to here. You should be close enough to the speaker to make eye contact if at all possible.

You will notice that some of your best listening takes place in one-on-one conversation. This is because most of the listening distractions or interferences I have been talking about are not present. Even if a large audience is present or you are at a large meeting (more than a dozen participants, for example), by positioning yourself close enough to engage in eye contact with the speaker, you simulate the conversational setting and reduce the level of environmental distraction.

Furthermore, if you can see the speaker's eyes and he or she can see yours, just as in conversation, it becomes highly difficult to tune out. This way you are virtually forced into paying attention, even if you might welcome a distraction or break from the subject at hand.

Take Brief Notes

Have you ever taken notes at a meeting or lecture only to throw them away later, even though they were quite detailed and required considerable effort to compile? If you have, it's likely that your notes lacked any kind of emphasis and, while voluminous, were incomplete.

With the exception of masters of shorthand, it's impossible for a note-taker to write down everything a speaker says. Any attempt to do so results in your writing while the speaker is still talking, which means you can't be fully listening because your perceptual focus is trying to produce an accurate written record.

Writing extended definitions also gives little clue as to the context of the material, or the speaker's degree of vocal emphasis. I recommend that you take notes to enhance listening and retention, but I also recommend that you do so sparingly, writing down key phrases or numbers, contextual notations (for example, "numbers cited refer to state government"), or questions to be asked later.

You should also have a way of denoting important items, such as a simple check mark. At the end of the presentation, you should end up with a brief summary of what was said in phrase form, with important items noted and a list of questions if appropriate.

Just as in preparing a speech outline, it is unimportant to write down the speaker's exact words. A list of his or her ideas in phrase form, as well as a knowledge of which ideas or pieces of information were emphasized, will suffice.

Enhancing Your Listening Environment

Be Aware of Your Own Expectations and Perceptions

If you anticipate that a speaker is going to make you angry or has been offensive in the past with other audiences, also be aware that effective listening will be more difficult if you do not resolve to "listen through" those aspects of the material you find problematical.

If terms or ideas are offensive or provocative in some other way, you might try writing down your expectations in advance as an ideas list and then making another ideas list during the speaker's presentation with the intention of comparing these ideas or areas of disagreement later. In this manner your listening will focus on the development of an ideas list, which will counteract your tendency to sit there waiting for the speaker to fulfill your negative expectations.

Be Idea Receptive

We have all been stuck at command-performance meetings, those at which your presence was politically expedient but otherwise a waste of your time—or so you thought.

The decision to attend but not participate, or to be only physically present, means that you will shut out the possibility of gaining any information of substance or use. You might be wrong, and you might never know it because you were not receptive. Once you have made the decision to attend a meeting or presentation, set aside the notion of how nonproductive you expect the session to be and listen receptively. Just as with the social occasion that you dreaded attending and ended up enjoying, meetings and presentations for which you harbor advance negative feelings can be surprisingly informative or useful if you remain idea receptive.

Ask the Right Question

Whenever possible or appropriate, ask questions of the speaker in any meeting. By the right questions, I mean three primary types:

1. *Repetition questions,* so that the speaker will review a statement or position
2. *Probe questions,* which enable you to examine the perspectives and background of the speaker's remarks

3. *Focus questions,* which ask the speaker for a better definition of what he or she considers most important for the
   listener to remember

Ask Repetition Questions

Questions that ask the speaker to review a part of his or her message
should be open ended and nonconfrontational. For example, your
question should be something like, "Would you review your remarks
regarding the need for a price increase?" rather than, "I don't see why
we need a price increase, could you go over your reasoning once
more?" With the open-ended repetition question, you will get a replay
of the material that is important to you without putting the speaker on
the defensive.

If the speaker resists, your response should be that you would like
the repetition for clarification. If you ask for clarification while
expressing your disagreement, you'll simply put the speaker on the
defensive and not get the same version of the information you are seeking to clarify.

Once again, your goal should be to heighten the retention of spoken material through effective listening rather than through confrontation. A defensive speaker is not as likely to help you achieve your
purpose of better understanding.

Ask Probe Questions

Probe questions are brief and to-the-point requests that ask for the
reasoning behind the statements. They should be directed toward
parts of the message you want to know more about, or to those areas
you feel the speaker has not fully explained. Such questions should be
open ended, such as, "What did you mean when you said 'our immediate environment?'"

Probe questions should be used to flesh out and amplify a speaker's
comment and to gain insight into the speaker's reasoning. Their use

can lessen the misunderstanding that can occur in any setting. Asking probe questions should be part of your job as an effective listener.

Ask Focus Questions

As the name implies, focus questions ask the speaker to get more specific and help you discern what the speaker considers most important. You will draw your own conclusions as to what was most important in any speaker's remarks, but these thoughts represent your perception and not those of the speaker.

The typical listener can always reiterate his or her own perceptions, but the truly effective listener is able to retain the message from the speaker's perspective as well.

Focus questions ask the speaker, "What aspect of your message is most important?" or "What do you believe to be the strongest or most compelling reason that we should adopt your plan?" or "Could you briefly summarize what you would like us to get out of your remarks?" With all these focus questions, you are asking the speaker to be specific in clarifying the aspects of the message he or she considered important.

In meetings, conferences, and negotiation sessions, the strategic use of repetition, probe, and focus questions should become an internalized method in enhancing your ability to listen.

Careful notation of a speaker's responses to your questions will also serve as a listening guide that is less a product of your own biases and more an accurate reflection of that speaker's intended message.

Summary

Although the vast emphasis in communication skills is on the delivery of the message, listening remains an important and usually overlooked part of the equation. Remove as many as possible of the physical and psychological barriers that surround any communicative encounter and enhance your retention by taking notes and asking the right questions.

Sharpening your listening skills with the techniques presented in this chapter will enable you to perform at a definite advantage whenever a precise recollection of what is said is important.

Quick Review:
Becoming a Better Listener

1. Understand that no one listens all the time.

2. Don't let your expectations cloud your ability to listen.

3. Avoid challenge-listening, in which you seek not to hear what's being said, but to build a case against the speaker.

4. You can't listen effectively if you're angry.

5. Don't "dismiss" a speaker because you think you know what he or she will say. (I call this automatic shutoff.)

6. Always sit near the speaker.

7. Take brief summary notes for later review.

8. Be idea receptive.

9. Ask questions.

10. Seek repetition of important points.

PART TWO

PREPARING AND DELIVERING POWERFUL SPEECHES AND PRESENTATIONS

CHAPTER FOUR

Speechwriting
How to Create a Powerful Message

AT-A-GLANCE SUMMARY

This chapter presents a step-by-step process for creating and writing
a successful, powerful speech, from selecting your topic to writing the
conclusion. You learn how to get and keep an audience on your side,
whether you are presenting a short message or a major address.

Among the words that strike fear in the hearts of many, ranking right up
there with the Internal Revenue Service's deceptively cheery and somehow
almost lyrical, "Dear Taxpayer, we have selected your return . . . ," are the
words, "We'd like you to give a speech on . . ."

Many of us barely hear the words that follow but slip instead into
the trance-like state we assume in the dentist's chair or at some other
moment of impending pain or displeasure. Our anxiety is not only
about getting up in front of an audience but also about assembling
some remarks that will dazzle them.

Many speakers start out aiming to dazzle and end up giving a highly
effective verbal sedative—not so much because creating a speech is all
that difficult but because it's an activity that most of us seldom perform. Thus we commit major errors and inefficiencies in the process,
leading to a poor product.

Why a Well-Structured Speech Is a Powerful Speech

It's a lot tougher to get a spoken message across to an audience than it
is to convey a written message. Anyone who sits down to read has just

decided to become a captive audience member. When someone reads an essay or even a novel, he or she has made a conscious decision to do so. The reader will adjust the light, find a comfortable chair, and even turn off the stereo in order to focus on the printed word. Listening to a speech is a much more passive process, in which you get to choose your level of attention, from total to none at all.

Readers are much more tolerant of boring or ill-constructed messages. How many times have you heard someone say of a novel, "I've read only fifty pages and I'm not quite sure what it's about"? Some of us (this writer excluded) even have the patience to finish an entire book and then say, "I really hated it."

Speakers don't have the luxury of tolerant audiences who will hang on to see if things get interesting. If your speech isn't interesting right away, you've lost much of your audience and won't get them back. Also, audiences don't arrange the speaking environment as they do the reading environment. Instead, it's done for them. And that environment is often filled with distractions—from uncomfortable chairs to rooms that are too hot or too cold, food being served (or not being served), other people coughing and sneezing, erratic sound systems, and so forth.

All of us can think faster than any speaker can talk. As described in Chapter 3, this sets up an inevitable cycle, referred to by communication theorists as "out-listening," a process in which we all engage while listening to a speaker. We tend to listen until we figure out what the speaker is saying, and then we let some distraction take over (Was that thunder? Did I close the car windows?). Next we drift back to the speaker to see if he or she is saying anything worthwhile. If the speech is well structured, we listen until the next distraction takes us in another direction. If the speech lacks definite structure, we won't be able to tune back in and are more likely to give up listening altogether.

The powerful speech—the one that holds the audience's attention—is not just the one that's well written or forcefully delivered (although those things help). The powerful spoken message is structured to compensate for distraction and the out-listening process. It is structured not just to capture and maintain audience attention but to let those who have wandered easily rejoin the speech in progress. By following the speechwriting steps in this chapter, you'll be better able to capture and hold the attention of your audience. Your audience will retain more of your message because your speech will be more likely to capture their immediate attention and let them know exactly which aspects of the topic you will be covering. Your speech will also let them know along the way where you are in your message and will provide a clear signal that you are ending your speech, so they can focus on your take-away message.

This chapter takes you through a step-by-step process that will eliminate or greatly reduce errors and inefficiencies and get you closer to dazzling your audience with the power of your message.

As You Begin . . .

First of all, don't sit over a yellow pad muttering or silently pondering the question over and over again, "What should I say first?" This is completely nonproductive and almost always results in hopelessly boring and usually insincere lines such as, "It is indeed an honor and a privilege to be here tonight to talk about . . ."

So for now, forget the question of what to say first (it will be covered later), and let's work on a more important beginning step . . .

Deciding What to Talk About

In some instances the topic may be predetermined by circumstances or necessity. Otherwise, topic selection can be the most time-consuming part of writing a speech—unless you first consider *what would you like to talk about?*

A constant goal of this book is to make you more comfortable and thus a more successful communicator. One key to comfort is actually having an interest in the topic you select. Can you talk to an audience effectively about a topic you don't like or believe in or don't know much about? Certainly, but it takes greater effort and is more difficult to research. In addition, your audience will sense your discomfort.

Step #1: Select the Topic

Begin your search for a topic by making a list of five to ten subjects you enjoy talking about, and then edit the list according to the following criteria.

How Long Do They Expect You to Speak?

Find out how much time will be available for your speech and select a topic accordingly. This will shorten your list considerably. Too many speakers select their topic by reasoning that they've talked about it before, and/or they still have their notes from the last time—the only problem being that the last time was a forty-five-minute sales presentation, and this is a ten-minute speech at a Rotary Club luncheon.

Consider the Audience

Look at your topic list in reference to these questions: What is the level of audience enthusiasm for your topic? Does the audience know more about the topic than you do? A good reason to choose another topic. Will your information be genuinely useful to them? Will it be information they have heard before?

Where to Find Speech Material

The Internet has become a major source of topic ideas and information, but the quality and credibility of the research and information available online varies widely. If you use the Internet, try to stick with sources you know to be reliable; otherwise, verify the accuracy of the information you use by checking several sources. The subject indexes at your local library are another good starting place for finding a speech topic. You can also find material from which to quote and come up with more speech ideas there. Another way to find speech topics is to scan the table of contents of a weekly news magazine. The articles are usually of interest to a wide segment of the public and are suitable for a similarly wide range of audiences. To develop your topic-idea list, jot down each article title or a phrase that summarizes the theme of the article.

Step #2: Write an Idea List

Once you have settled on a speech topic, take your topic idea and free-associate with it. This means writing down a list of topics that come to mind as you think about your probable topic. Keep your list brief, in word or phrase form—it should contain at least ten but not more than twenty items.

The reason for the wide latitude in the length of your idea list is that some topics are easier to develop than others. For example, scientific or highly technical ideas are likely to be highly limited in scope, whereas general topics would produce a longer list.

I have set an upper limit of the idea list at twenty because, in my experience, once an idea list gets any longer than this, the ideas become too distant from the original topic to be useful in creating your speech.

Here is an example of the idea list I generated on the topic "acid rain":

- Cloud content
- Dead trees
- Other causes
- Cars
- Specific evidence
- Clean Air Act
- Individual responses

- Paint damage
- Greenhouse effect
- Measuring acid rain
- Acid rain defined
- Power plants
- International sources
- Corporate responsibility

Warning: the idea list can sometimes produce an idea that causes you to change your entire topic. For example, in the preceding list I came up with the idea "greenhouse effect," which might easily be a topic unto itself.

If you spot an idea on your list that you'd like to talk about more than your original topic, just generate an idea list using that new idea as a starting point, and you're on your way to a better speech than you originally planned.

Step #3: Choose Your Showcase Idea

Review your idea list, and choose the idea that, above all others, you want to get across to your audience. I call this the *showcase idea,* because it is the idea to which all the other parts of your talk will point, just like spotlights in a showcase.

For example, although I started out with the general topic, acid rain, I decided that the topic was in need of definition, and that became my showcase idea: to define what acid rain is. Once you have chosen your showcase idea, write it down in phrase or sentence form. In this case, the showcase idea would be: "What exactly is acid rain?"

Step #4: Choose Your Spotlight Ideas

Spotlight ideas support your showcase idea by supplying further information that points toward or illuminates your showcase idea. So your next step is to choose two, three, or even four ideas that support or are most closely related to your showcase idea and list them. The number depends on two factors:

1. *The complexity of the topic.* Since some topics are more difficult to explain, you may want to limit yourself to two spotlight ideas. If your topic is easily understood, you may want to choose three or four spotlight ideas.
2. *The amount of time available for the speech.* Simply stated, the more spotlight ideas, the longer the speech. A typical

speech with one showcase idea and two or three spotlight ideas will last anywhere from five to seven minutes once the beginning and ending are added.

To build an even longer speech, add another showcase idea and another set of spotlight ideas. Using this system, you can easily and systematically create a speech of a half hour or longer. Writing even a lengthy speech becomes a matter of creating a series of smaller units instead of the unmanageable task it seemed at first.

Step #5: Write the Text or Body of Your Speech

To begin creating the text of your speech, write the idea that you most want to get across to your audience—the *showcase idea*—in sentence form. Next, write down each of your spotlight ideas (ideas that support or amplify the showcase idea) and construct a brief essay on each spotlight idea (about 250 words).

Here is an example of how a speech on acid rain would look after following these *exact* steps (note that it is numbered II, because this is actually the middle of the speech):

II. Showcase Idea:

A full appreciation of the effects of acid rain on our environment begins with an understanding of exactly what acid rain is. Acid rain is defined as . . .

Spotlight Idea #1. Sources of acid rain

Now that you know what acid rain is, the next logical question is: Where does it come from? While some acidity may occur in nature, we make the rest of it! That's right—the major source of man-made acid rain is found in sulfur dioxide emissions (SO_2), from the burning of fossil fuels, especially high-sulfur coal. Other ways we produce acid rain include . . .

Spotlight Idea #2. Acid rain affects you personally
Just because you can't see it doesn't mean it isn't there. Acid rain
affects everything from the finish on your car to the size of your
electric bill. Let's talk about car finishes.

If you are creating a speech that is entirely scripted, this series of
brief essays, all of which highlight your showcase idea, will make up the
body of your talk. A good rule of thumb is to have a minimum of two
to a maximum of four spotlight ideas per showcase idea. A speech can
also have more than one showcase idea, but if you get beyond two or
three, remember that you run the risk of losing the focus that allows an
audience to come away with a specific message. Aside from time constraints, the complexity of the topic and the attention span of your
audience should be the major factors determining the number of
showcase and supporting spotlight ideas your speech will contain.

By following the steps outlined here and keeping in mind that the
average speaker talks at about 125 words per minute, you should be
able to plan the length of your speech with some precision. (In planning the length of your talk, don't forget to allow time for a question-
and-answer session when appropriate or expected.)

If you prefer to deliver the speech from an outline instead of a
script, I still recommend that you script the showcase idea (a part of the
speech that you'll want to get *exactly* right) and then list a few key
phrases for each spotlight idea.

Here is how such an outline might look for the topic "acid rain":

II. Showcase Idea:
A full appreciation of the effects of acid rain on our environ-
ment begins with an understanding of just what acid rain is.
Acid rain is defined as . . .

Spotlight Idea #1. Sources of acid rain
• SO$_2$ emissions
• Fossil-fuel combustion
• Auto emissions
• High-sulfur coal
• Natural sources

Spotlight Idea #2. How acid rain affects you
• Auto finishes
• Drinking water
• Plant life
• The economy

Text versus Outline

The question of whether to use a script or an outline should be answered by your level of experience as a speaker and by your knowledge of the topic. Once you have practiced and familiarized yourself with a scripted speech, you may wish to convert it to outline form.

In preparing an outline based on your script, include key phrases as I have done here, but also be sure to include any pieces of information you have a hard time remembering, such as names, dates, formulas, or statistics. The outline should be used to keep your ideas on track and in sequence. Generally, the more you know about the topic and the more familiar you are with your script, the less information you'll need on your outline.

Step #6: Write the Introduction

Now that you have completed the middle or body of your speech, you'll have a considerable advantage in writing an introduction because you now know most of what you are going to say. Most speakers fail to realize the crucial nature of an introduction in getting an audience focused and on their side. The introduction should be viewed as a sort of verbal curtain you draw back to reveal your showcase idea. Your job as a speechwriter at this point is to make the audience wonder what's behind the curtain.

Get to Them Right Away

In that first moment, you have the unique advantage in that everyone is focused on you and your forthcoming message. It is important to get to your audience immediately in order to maximize attention to and retention of your message. As you begin your speech, don't waste your time and theirs with such words as, "Today I am going to speak about . . ." You're standing at a podium facing an audience and everyone present can surmise that you're going to talk about something. So dispense with the typical bland opening words and begin your message immediately.

Set the Emotional Tone

Do you want your audience to be amused? Relieved? Guilty? Anxious? Or even angry? Emotional tone is set by language, so choose language in keeping with the emotional tone you want to set.

For example, in a talk on environmental issues you might begin by saying: "Every member of this audience is guilty of a crime . . ." and then continue to talk about some of the negative impacts that all of us have on the environment. With this statement, you have certainly gotten the attention of those in your audience, and you may even have startled them a bit with your controversial opening statement.

The emotional goal of your introduction should suit *your* purposes. Usually a speaker attempts to write and deliver a feel-good or a "warm and fuzzy" introduction. If an amiable opening suits the speech or the audience, go ahead, but remember that you'll be sacrificing memorability.

In addition to setting the emotional tone of your speech and building audience interest, the major purpose of the introduction is to lead the listener to your showcase idea.

Continuing my "Every member of this audience is guilty of a crime" statement, I could then introduce my showcase idea—defining acid rain: "But it is easy to see how you could be guilty of a crime when you don't have any understanding of it. I am referring to acid rain, an environmental problem to which we all contribute, whether we are aware of it or not. Acid rain is . . ."

Types of Introductions

Following are some specific types of speech introductions to use as a guide in writing an introduction for your speech, along with some tips on how to make them work for you.

QUOTATIONS Use a quotation when you come across something so moving or irresistibly clever that you have to include it in your opening remarks. It should imply that you are well read and have done some research to unearth a particular pearl of wisdom for the delight of your audience. This may or may not be true, but it's the impression your audience will get with the use of a well-selected quotation.

A couple of cautions about using quotations: first and foremost, get it right and double-check it from a reliable source. Having a quotation "just a little bit off" will undo any positive impressions you had hoped to make by using it in the first place. Also, don't overintroduce a quote with statements such as, "With his usual degree of eloquence, the late and great statesman Adlai E. Stevenson once moved an audience by telling them . . ." Such long-winded phrases prior to a quotation diminish its impact by reducing any element of surprise that existed.

Either open with the quotation itself, followed by a brief phrase such as, "With these words, Adlai Stevenson . . ." or, if you want to use the author's name up front, say: "Adlai Stevenson once said . . ."

Second, *don't ever use someone else's words or wit as your own without an acknowledgment.* Even if you do so inadvertently, the damage to your credibility can be severe. If someone finds out, *and they will,* the whole purpose of your message is likely to be obscured in the oft-justified furor that results from the appearance of plagiarism.

If you choose to begin your speech with a quotation, be certain to avoid the obvious. For example, you don't want to find yourself speaking to a group of historians and beginning with an obvious statement such as, "'Four score and seven years ago'—with these words a great American president . . ."; or before a group of baseball fans, quoting Yogi Berra's endearing but hopelessly overused "It ain't over till it's over."

The use of quotations should reveal you to be a speaker of diligence and insight who has the generosity of spirit to recognize that others may have had interesting thoughts on your subject even before you did.

ILLUSTRATIVE STORIES In this world of scripts and teleprompters and presentations littered with slick computer-generated graphics, it is always refreshing to hear a speaker say, "Before I begin my remarks, I'd like to tell you a story." Perhaps it's a collective wish to return to a simpler time, but it's a line that invariably commands an audience's attention.

The first rule at a moment like this is to captivate, not to disappoint. Your story should be dramatic or touching, if that suits your purpose, and memorable to the extent that those present will want to repeat it.

Your story should brief, as a general rule not much more than 10 percent of the length of your talk, and should have a direct link to your topic. Otherwise, the main reason you are there, to give a speech, becomes obscured by the entertainment provided by your story.

Following is an example of an illustrative story used at the beginning of a speech on corporate citizenship.

Just before last Christmas, a woman came into our central billing office with a cash payment for an overdue electric bill. As the bedraggled customer counted out the last of the $123.83 owed us, she made it known that this was her children's Christmas fund—but she wanted to start the holiday season with her debts paid.

Our representative asked the woman to wait in the reception area for a few minutes. Right there and then he took up a collection in the office and returned that mom's Christmas money—a spontaneous gift from our employer to someone in need.

More than our organized community activities and planned events I'll be telling you about, that moment tells you the kind of people we are at American United Power and why I am proud . . .

And so the illustrative story introduces the idea that American United Power is a good corporate citizen.

A question that arises with regard to an illustrative story is whether it needs to reflect an actual event or can be something you simply composed. The answer is either. While you may wish to use an event from your own experience, sometimes modifying or even embellishing a story can increase its impact. You may also want to modify a story to obscure the identity of its participants.

If you find yourself adjusting the content of an illustrative story or even creating one, it's important that you not mislead your audience. Use words such as, "While the characters in my story may not be real, what happened to them has happened to all of us at one time or another . . ." or "While I've changed that story a bit, it still represents . . ."

Otherwise, especially in an adversarial situation, be assured that someone will track down your story and attempt to prove it false. If your illustrative story is modified or fictional, make sure you say so.

SPUR-OF-THE-MOMENT REMARKS The so-called spur-of-the-moment or off-the-cuff remark can be an effective device. I say so-called because such spontaneity requires careful planning. Here are some typical kinds of remarks:

1. A little known fact about the group to which you are speaking
2. A complimentary reference to your host
3. A reference to a very recent and/or very topical news event

Perhaps the best summary of how to handle spur-of-the-moment remarks is the story of Winston Churchill, who, when asked the secret of his ability to make spontaneous remarks with such ease and eloquence, responded, "I practice them!"

DEFINITIONS OF KEY TERMS If you don't have time to hunt down the perfect quote, or are uncomfortable making spur-of-the-moment remarks, you might consider defining a term to start your speech.

Far from a last resort, this device is particularly effective with a more sophisticated audience and works well if your talk is centered on a complex technical topic or a term that is often mentioned but seldom defined.

One cautionary note: if you choose to open with a definition, be careful as to its source. Is the source well recognized and/or respected by the audience, or will the source of the definition merely stir up controversy?

If you choose to use your own definition, with yourself as the source, do so because you have sufficient authority to arrive at your own definition. Otherwise, it looks as if you are going your own way because you had neither the time nor the ability to do more.

RHETORICAL QUESTIONS The rhetorical question presents a prime opportunity for one of the more awkward moments in public speaking. We have all heard speakers begin with questions such as, "How many of you have thought of visiting a tiny Caribbean island on your next vacation?"

There are a couple of flaws in this approach. The first is that *this* and *all* rhetorical questions, by their nature, create a moment of conflict as the audience wonders whether you want an answer to the question, a raised hand, or a polite affirmative nod. In those crucial opening seconds, when you should be capturing the undivided attention of your audience, you have confused them.

Aside from the momentary awkwardness, there is another danger, illustrated by the lawyer's old dictum about never asking a question to which you don't already know the answer. If the question is met with blank stares, or only four of two hundred hands are hesitantly raised, you have just unwittingly made it apparent to all present that most of your audience doesn't care about your topic. With your own introductory words, you have created an uphill battle.

If you insist on the rhetorical question as an introduction, make sure that you are totally sure of your audience's response.

ANECDOTES Another type of introduction for the risk-takers among us is telling an anecdote or funny story. This can be highly effective— but whether you want to use it is a judgment call, with this author voting in the negative. I realize that some kind of joke is customary and even expected at the beginning of certain types of speeches. In such cases, I'd keep the story short.

If you *must* begin your talk with a witticism, don't make the mistake of telling your audience that you'll begin with a funny story. Part of the key to getting a laugh is the element of surprise, which you will have sacrificed if you let an audience know your intentions.

Assuming you have a choice, I advise against beginning your speech with an anecdote, for several reasons. First of all, humor has an incredible capacity to amuse, but it has an even greater capacity to offend. As one who has spoken in public for thousands of hours, I am still amazed at the ability of the listener to misconstrue a remark, take it completely out of context, and take offense.

Second, there is always the possibility that your funny story will be a dud. This has happened to most of us, and it doesn't feel good. Public humiliation is a horrible feeling, be it in front of an audience of six or six hundred.

On the other hand, if your anecdote is received with thunderous gales of laughter, at some point—assuming your purpose is other than to deliver a comic monologue—you are reduced to saying something like, "and now to be serious . . . ," a line guaranteed to get any listener to tune you out.

How Long an Introduction?   Depending on the duration and depth of your speech, your introduction should last anywhere from 1½ minutes for a five- to seven-minute speech to 3 or 4 minutes for a speech of fifteen minutes or longer.

In the introduction to a longer speech with more than one showcase idea, be sure that you inform your audience that you will be covering several aspects of the topic. Mention each of your showcase ideas in the introduction. This way an audience is prepared for a longer speech and has a good idea of where you're going throughout the speech.

Here is an example of an introduction to a longer speech with multiple showcase ideas:

> For most of us, understanding anything about the national debt is right up there with quantum mechanics when it comes to making sense of the issue. But I think I can make the dismal science come alive or at least make it personal for you by looking at one subject from three distinct points of view: first, why the numbers keep getting larger; second, what they mean to each and every one here today; and finally, a novel solution that may just make this coming crisis go away!

The point is to accomplish the purposes of an introduction— getting attention, setting the emotional tone, and introducing the showcase idea—without overshadowing the message itself.

Step #7: Write Your Conclusion

Speeches have been compared with relationships in that they are easy enough to begin but exceedingly difficult to end, or at least to end gracefully. I have often seen speakers end with a shrug, or by limply asking the host, "Can I sit down now?" In such cases, the speech hasn't ended; the speaker has just given up. By following a few simple steps, you can easily avoid such awkward moments and bring your speech to a smooth, successful conclusion.

Beginning the Ending

Since audiences tend to tune in and out during any speech, you'll want to provide a strong indicator that they should tune back in for the ending.

The best way to do so is with a concluding marker phrase that can vary widely but is typified by the ever popular but overused, "In conclusion . . ." If you're stuck, that's okay, but do try to use a variation of this phrase for your concluding marker. Here are a few examples:

"As you can see from what I've said . . ."

"The remarks I've made today point in one direction . . ."

"I've enjoyed speaking with you today, and as I conclude, there is one particular point I'd like you to think about . . ."

These concluding marker phrases are significant to your audience because each one of them refers to your message in the past tense. Once you begin with that marker phrase, don't mislead them by introducing new information.

How Long a Conclusion?

You shouldn't talk for more than two additional minutes if your talk is less than fifteen minutes long, nor more than three if your talk is more than fifteen minutes long. If you go any longer at this point, you'll lose your audience and your impact.

Writing the Conclusion

Many speakers seem to hit the wall creatively as they finish writing the last spotlight idea in the body of their speech. Your conclusion is too important and too memorable a part of your speech to throw away, so do some serious thinking and writing at this point. A strong conclusion will increase the memorability and impact of your speech, whereas a weak one will greatly diminish the effectiveness of your message.

Start your conclusion with a beginning marker phrase and make certain that your final words accomplish one of the following goals:

1. *Summarize the showcase idea(s) of your speech.*
Example: "In my look at the AIDS epidemic today, I have considered three areas: treatment, counseling, and research. With the information I have provided, you can readily see the very clear need for . . ."

2. *Repeat and reinforce the spotlight point that you would most like remembered.*
Example: "Although I've covered several aspects of the AIDS epidemic, I'd like each and every one of you to remember that until we are closer to a cure, counseling people with AIDS remains an area of utmost importance."

3. *When possible or appropriate, a good technique in concluding a speech is to refer back to or repeat a part of your introduction.*

Example: "As I said in the beginning, Dr. Helen Caldecott's statement on the horror of nuclear war that 'the living will envy the dead' is no exaggeration. I hope that I have left each of you with a deeper understanding of how her words only begin to describe this peril."

Using Linkage Words

In addition to the concluding marker phrases, a minor but important part of the speech-writing process is to insert so-called linkage or transitional phrases at various parts of your now completely written speech. These are words that bring you from one part of the speech to the next—from introduction to showcase idea, from showcase to spotlight idea, and from the final spotlight idea to your conclusion.

For example, from the introduction to the showcase idea, a linkage word might be "specifically" or the phrase "to be specific." From one spotlight idea to the next, a linkage phrase might be an ordinal phrase such as, "first of all," or "second," or "another point you should remember . . ."

Such phrases are used naturally by the experienced speaker because they make so much sense in organizing the speech, both for the speaker and the audience. They are also easy to forget, however, because they are not usually considered a part of the speech itself. Linkage words and phrases serve as signals for your audience that you are about to make another point. They function as a kind of verbal strobe light that will, we hope, recapture anyone's wandering attention.

To help your speech flow smoothly, linkage words and phrases should be inserted at the following places in the text of your speech:

1. After your introduction, just before the showcase idea
2. At the beginning of each spotlight idea
3. At the start of your conclusion

Here are some effective linkage words and phrases:

• Specifically
• First of all, second, and so on
• Another important point
• Most important
• Above all, remember that . . .
• Let's examine another issue.
• I'll leave you with this thought . . .
• As I wrap things up . . .

The Final Word

Consistent with the viewpoint that a speech should be looked at essentially as an organized conversation, the last words of your speech should contain nothing more than a simple statement such as, "I've enjoyed talking with you today, and I look forward to meeting you again." Use some variation of this as your final words—thank the audience for inviting you, and then *stop talking!*

Summary

A good speech is best written from the middle. Start by choosing a topic and creating an idea list, generated by jotting down any phrases you can think of related to that topic. From that list of between ten and twenty ideas, select the one that is of most interest to you and thus most likely to interest your audience. That is your showcase idea or take-away message.

Next, select two (or three, depending on the complexity of your topic and the length of your speech) ideas that support your showcase idea. These are your spotlight ideas. Once you assemble a brief essay for the showcase and spotlight ideas, you have the middle or body of your speech.

Of course, you can't create an introduction before you know what you are going to say, but once you have that information it's time to go back and write the introduction. The key to a powerful introduction is to grab the attention of your audience right away and make every word count. Forget the usual "Today I am going to talk about . . . " You've just been introduced and you're standing at a podium! They know you're going to say something. For maximum impact, open with a startling statement, an amazing quote, or a piece of information they didn't know about, and use it to spark their interest in what is to follow.

Finally, write a compelling conclusion that will leave your audience inspired and with a clear idea of your point. Begin with a transitional phrase (e.g., "In conclusion . . ."), repeat your showcase idea, and, if it fits, repeat a piece of the quotation or startling statement with which you began your speech. Then thank your listeners, and exit to thunderous applause. If you follow these suggestions for building a truly powerful message, that applause will be much more likely!

Quick Review:
Creating a Powerful Message

1. A well-delivered, well-received speech begins with a topic that is of definite interest to you and possible interest to your audience.

2. Grab audience attention immediately, with your first words.

3. Humorous introductions usually work against you, even if you get a laugh.

4. Don't use quotations to seem learned; use them because they work!

5. Don't ever use someone else's words without acknowledgment.

6. Define key terms even if most of your audience already understands them. (Some of those present may not.)

7. Don't open your speech with a question; sometimes you get an answer you weren't expecting.

8. Arrange your ideas so that you finish up on your most important one. (Audiences tend to remember what they heard last.)

9. Once you say words such as, "In conclusion," don't talk any longer than two minutes more.

10. Check your outline for linkage words, the phrases that lead you from one part of your speech to the next.

CHAPTER FIVE

Audience Analysis
Making Sure Your Message Hits Home

AT-A-GLANCE SUMMARY
This chapter helps you to tailor your remarks to a specific audience, a frequently overlooked way to dramatically increase the impact of your message.

The importance of considering and including each specific audience while creating a speech cannot be overstated. If you make the mistake of so many speakers and ignore your particular audience by simply delivering a generic, non-audience-specific message, your audience will return the favor by ignoring or quickly forgetting about you and what you had to say. On the other hand, if you take into account such factors as demographics, issues, perspectives, and interests as you prepare and deliver a speech, the audience will return the favor with attention to and retention of your remarks.

Matching the Topic to the Audience

Even before you begin the task of including the audience, you should consider whether your topic is compatible. For example, even the most eloquent among us would be hard pressed to deliver an attention-grabbing talk on the latest trends in midwifery practice to a group of senior citizens or one on recent changes in deep-sea fishing technology to a group of Midwestern corn farmers. In either case, the audience would most likely respond with bewildered stares followed by a collective yawn, no matter how artfully your talk was crafted.

Advertising professionals perform extensive research in order to define exactly who will buy their product, and they adjust such elements as the look, content, and language of their advertising to appeal to a specific audience. Thus they avoid wasting advertising dollars on audiences who don't care about their product or message or may even be offended by it.

Ignoring audience demographics can be especially embarrassing. A couple of decades ago the now defunct National Airlines decided to sell travel from New York City to Florida and chose to do so with posters in the New York City subways. They thought this would be a good way to reach commuters as they scurried about in the bleakness of a New York winter.

That, however, is where National's thinking about its audience stopped. The posters were large, simple, and offensive. Huge block letters trumpeted the words: "BOY, ARE YOU PALE!!!" and in much smaller letters at the bottom of the poster, "A Reminder from National Airlines."

No sooner did the ads appear than minority groups expressed their contempt for the designation "Boy" and the highly inaccurate reference to their skin color. National goofed by ignoring the racial composition of its audience and paid the price by having to scrap an expensive ad campaign.

It's unlikely you'll have to scrap your speech, but you should examine the demographics or unique characteristics of your audience, to make your remarks audience specific.

Making Sure You Mention Your Audience

The first step in tailoring your remarks to an audience is to mention that group, by name, within your speech. Whenever possible, include the mention in your introduction, so the speech presents both the appearance and the reality that it was created specifically for that audience.

For example, instead of saying, "Our national debt is considered by some to be a time bomb that can be defused only if we have the courage to . . . ," the same line delivered in an audience-centered manner would be as follows:

> I am particularly heartened to be delivering this message to this group of accounting and finance professionals because you, as the sentinels of our nation's economic health, are in the best position to understand that the national debt is considered by some to be a time bomb that can be defused only if . . .

Even if your audience doesn't have a direct relationship to your topic, you can still include them in your remarks. For example, here is the same opening delivered to another audience:

> As senior citizens, you have the advantage of long experience and the perspective that comes with it. Thus, each of you has a special capacity to understand that the national debt is a virtual time bomb that can be defused only . . .

Adjusting the Emphasis and Content to Various Audiences

In delivering a talk on effective résumé writing to a group of recent college graduates, your speech would be more audience centered if you emphasized the virtues of community service and volunteer work to compensate for lack of formal experience. The same speech delivered to a midcareer audience might stress how to construct the objectives statement and minimize the community-service area.

Deciding on Your Target Audience

This step is a matter of anticipating what the demographic profile of your audience will be and modifying your speech to include that target audience. The goal is to increase the impact of your message by making your communication more intimate, giving your audience the impression that you are really talking to each of them.

Following are some major demographic factors and audience characteristics you should consider in targeting your message, along with some samples of how to make a speech more audience centered.

Consider the Age of an Audience

Is the audience composed of or concentrated in a particular age group? The very old and the very young are less likely to be receptive to complex or convoluted messages.

With any audience, check to see if your examples are contemporary. For example, the death of John F. Kennedy was a dark, unforgettable moment in history for many and can be mentioned to evoke a sense of national loss and tragedy. Since it happened decades ago, however, it is as distant a memory as the Great Depression to others and has little if any emotional significance to younger audiences.

Without being patronizing ("I've got a really far-out talk for you today!"), be aware of the language and concerns of your audience that may be related to age. You may wish to make references to the popular music or literature of your audience, but do so only when it's relevant and appropriate. Also, if referring to any aspect of the audience's pop culture, avoid the intergenerational temptation to make the kind of critical or humorous comment that will needlessly offend rather than draw your listeners close to you and your message.

Finally, don't refer to any age gap that may exist between you and your audience. Your appearance will have done that for you, and further commentary on how young or how old the speaker or audience is will be construed as a sign of your own discomfort, possibly increasing the psychological distance between you and your audience.

Consider the Educational Level of an Audience

It has long been my contention that education doesn't make you any smarter, but it can improve your critical and analytical ability. An educated audience may be more receptive to new ideas but less tolerant of inaccuracy, poorly developed reasoning, or evidence of poor research.

Credentials are also important to more educated audiences. Your position and qualifications are more likely to be on the minds of such audiences and should be dealt with early in your message.

If your credentials don't compare with those of the audience you face, don't try to compensate with terminology you wouldn't normally use, in an attempt to "speak their language," just to show that you can. Also avoid making humorous references to the impressive credentials held by an audience. Both tactics will be perceived as hostile and will serve to create an issue where there was none before.

Don't be intimidated by an audience that seems more qualified than you are. Remember that you would not have been asked to speak unless those who selected you felt you had a worthwhile message to deliver.

Consider the Occupation of Your Audience

When your audience is composed almost exclusively of one occupational group, your message and illustrative examples can gain immediate and increased acceptance if they refer directly to that audience.

For example, if you're talking to airline pilots, an example or topic related to the importance of adherence to procedure or safety is likely to be well received because airline pilots rely on both these areas for the successful practice of their profession. Similarly, sharing a positive travel experience is always welcomed by pilots because these highly trained professionals more often hear about missing luggage than they do about smooth, safe travel.

If you're speaking to a group of rheumatologists, examples or topics involving senior citizens would be welcome because this is the primary population served by this medical specialty, just as pediatricians would be more attentive to examples or topics involving children.

In relating to occupational activity, refer either to the activity itself or to the population served by that occupational group (e.g., senior citizens and rheumatologists or children and pediatricians). By looking in each of these directions, you widen the sources of examples that get your speech closer to your audience.

When faced with an audience composed of people with similar professional backgrounds, be they lawyers, accountants, or engineers, some speakers choose to tell one of the tired old jokes we have all heard a jillion times. (How can you tell the number of engineers in a room? Add up the number of white socks and divide by two!) Avoid such turkeys. Your audience has heard them, and if you're lucky enough not to have offended them, you've done little more than reveal yourself as a dullard and a keeper of tired humor.

Consider Organizational Affiliations

Here is an easy way to get you and your message closer to your audience that speakers often miss.

If your organization happens to be the local chapter of Rotarians, Lions, or Jaycees, or any organization that has a long tradition of community service, don't miss the opportunity to recognize their contributions even before getting to your speech. You have just enhanced the audience's receptivity to your message.

If you're speaking to a group other than a service organization, you might refer instead to their long history (which you looked up ahead of time) or prominent members who might be present (which you checked in advance).

Such audience references, which you can find with minimal investigation, indicate that you are a sensitive and caring communicator and, at least for the time you'll be talking to them, as close to one of their own as you can get. Direct and positive references to an audience or organization can quickly move your listeners from holding a neutral position to being very much on your side.

Consider the Racial or Ethnic Makeup of Your Audience

Consider both your own and your audience's racial or ethnic makeup. When it's possible to use examples or pay compliments to an ethnically or racially based organization, by all means do so; to ignore such realities, particularly if you are of a different background from that of the group, can be considered a snub.

If you are paying compliments to a group, do some research to acquaint yourself with such information as prominent members who might be present, or special occasions or holidays observed by that group that coincide with or even approximate the date of your appearance. Leaders of such groups or those responsible for booking your appearance will be helpful in getting you this information and will genuinely appreciate that you bothered to ask.

Remember that the major purpose of mentioning an audience specifically within your talk or acknowledging their accomplishments is to involve them more directly in your message and thus increase its impact. Don't let your words of praise become so lengthy as to obscure your message. In short, recognize, but don't patronize.

Particularly in these times of increased ethnic and racial pride and sensitivity, recognition of anything from an accomplishment to a struggle to overcome past and present obstacles is helpful in building a rapport with your audience. Avoid the trap, however, that nonmembers of an ethnic or racial group fall into with remarks such as "I feel your pain/joy." As an outsider, the fact is you don't, and you haven't shared their experience. Pretending to do so will be perceived as patronizing to the point of offensiveness. The rule is worth repeating: recognize, don't patronize!

Consider the Economic Status of Your Audience

This is not an attempt to get into a debate about whether the rich are different, but a recognition of the fact that there are differences both in economic status across audiences and in levels of understanding when it comes to financial matters and terminology.

On the matter of economic status, be attuned to your audience and use examples to which they can readily relate. For example, in speaking about such matters as average incomes, the mention of six-figure salaries in front of an audience that has never earned that much money or has little prospect of doing so will signal that you may be out of touch with your listeners' lives. Make sure your economic examples use numbers and situations with which your audience can readily identify.

Also, when using financial and economic terminology, make sure that the audience is likely to know what you are talking about. Most of us know that the "S&P 500" is not an automobile race, but terms such as "dollar-cost averaging" and "accelerated depreciation" can cause the eyes of many supposedly financially sophisticated audiences to glaze over.

Consider the Gender of Your Audience

Some of you may think that considering audience gender distribution is going a bit too far, but those of you who do probably need this information the most.

I refer particularly to speeches given before women's groups. We have a sexist language that is generally dominated by male pronouns. Therefore, when we use examples that refer to "the best attorney" or "the most skilled surgeon," our language usually tricks us into referring to either of these accomplished individuals as a male ("If the most skilled surgeon were to evaluate this case, *he* would undoubtedly agree that . . ."). I'd suggest that you amend all such statements to include both male and female pronouns (" . . . *he or she* would undoubtedly agree that . . .").

While this small linguistic adjustment may seem cumbersome at first, it will impress your audience with your sensitivity to such issues. And a failure to do so may offend female members of some audiences. Watch your pronouns.

Checklist

Use the Audience Profile Checklist below in preparing a speech to make sure you tailor your remarks to each specific audience.

AUDIENCE PROFILE CHECKLIST/SURVEY

☐ What is the gender of your audience?

_____ Male _____ Female _____ Both

☐ What is their approximate average age? _____

☐ What is their approximate age range? _____

☐ What is the marital status of your audience?

_____ Married _____ Single _____ Divorced

☐ Are there any unique cultural / ethnic audience characteristics?

_____

☐   What is their educational background?

_____ High School _____ College
_____ Graduate degrees

☐   What is the religious affiliation of your audience?

_____

☐   What is the professional occupation of your audience?

_____

☐   What is the political perspective of your audience?

_____

☐   What is their salary range?

_____ $10,000–$20,000

_____ $20,000–$40,000

_____ $40,000–$70,000

_____ $70,000–$100,000

_____ $100,000+

☐   Is your audience a fraternal or sorietal organization?

_____

☐   Are you speaking on the occasion of an anniversary or the celebration of an accomplishment or award?

☐   Are there famous or notable people and/or members present who should be acknowledged?

Summary

I've included this chapter because it describes an area too many speakers ignore. The occasional or inexperienced speaker has a natural tendency to treat the whole speech preparation process as a self- rather than an audience-centered performance activity. Yet just a bit of attention spent on some of the details covered in this chapter can pay huge dividends in terms of audience appreciation of and attention to your message.

Be sure to include your audience in your speech. Think about their demographics, interests, and opinions and include them in your remarks. Make specific mention of your audience. Including each audience within your speech, often by just a mention of their concerns, issues, or perspectives, is a simple step too many teachers neglect. One of the biggest compliments you can receive after a speech is the comment, "You were really talking to us." Tailoring a speech along the lines of the information presented in this chapter is the surest way to elicit that comment.

Quick Review:
Audience Analysis

1. Make sure there are specific references to your audience in your speech.
2. When speaking to an organization, know its history and recent accomplishments and include them in your remarks.
3. Not all topics are suitable for all audiences.
4. Be careful of generation gaps in choosing your illustrative examples.
5. Don't be intimidated by audiences with greater credentials than yours.

6. Avoid stereotypic humor, especially in speaking to professional groups.

7. Be attentive to such audience demographics as age, educational level, ethnicity, and so forth.

8. Refer to individual audience members by name.

9. Recognize differing levels of familiarity with your topic, in the same audience.

10. If you are a nonmember of a minority group to whom you are speaking, don't patronize them with "I feel your pain" remarks.

CHAPTER SIX

Handling Tough Questions and Tough Audiences

AT-A-GLANCE SUMMARY

This chapter is about handling tough questions and audiences. Although the primary focus is the question-and-answer period that follows a speech, the techniques covered are applicable to any Q&A situation, from the job or media interview to the witness stand.

In the pages that follow, you'll learn how to correct commonly made errors and how to avoid questioner traps.

This is not a chapter about evading tough questions. You should face the fact that the best way to handle tough questions is to answer them. In that spirit, this chapter provides a systematic approach to answering the questions of an audience or an interviewer effectively while expressing your informational agenda on target issues.

"And now I'd be happy to take your questions." If there are any insincere words contained in this book, you have just read them. After you've conquered the demons of speaker anxiety and prepared, rehearsed, and delivered a most masterful piece of oratory, you often have to invite audience questions. At this point, most of us would rather be home trying to teach our cat to fetch.

Q&A sessions in the form of press conferences present such a significant degree of risk that presidents often avoid them under the guise of seeming "presidential." Politicians of all levels and stripes avoid spontaneous Q&A sessions so they can maintain control of a carefully honed image rather than have it shattered by an errant response.

The Q&A session that follows a speech means giving up control of the situation. It also means the audience will see a version of you without the safety net of a prepared text or outline—a glimpse of the real you. If you handle the Q&A session poorly, you could make a spectacular blunder, inadvertently offend, forget the obvious, or even reveal yourself as someone who doesn't know as much as your audience initially thought you did.

But don't panic; you can exercise a lot more control over the Q&A session than you realize. In fact, if properly handled, even if you don't know the answer to *every* question (speakers worry about that), the Q&A session can become a real asset and positive contribution to your communicative image and impact.

By using the strategies presented in this chapter and making an honest attempt to answer the questions an audience may have for you, you can come out of the Q&A session as a more authoritative and credible communicator.

Establishing Ground Rules to Maintain Control

You might fear the Q&A session because you feel you are giving up control of the situation. But that's only partially true. Some ways you can gain greater control of the Q&A session follow.

Set the Length of the Session

This is done with ease and subtlety by saying, "I have a limited amount of time to take some questions from the audience." Notice that you have said "some" questions and a "limited" amount of time. The choice of these words is intentional. By saying "some questions" you have implied that the session will not go on until *every* query has been answered. Also, by saying you have a "limited amount of time" without specifying it, you get to determine what that interval will be.

This way you can conclude the session at your discretion by again saying that your time is limited and you're wrapping up. If the Q&A

session is going extraordinarily well, you may wish to let it continue longer than planned.

Allow One Question per Person

Another important ground rule to set up *before* the Q&A session is to limit questions to one per person until everyone present has had an opportunity to ask a question. This rule seems like the height of fairness and makes you look good; more important, it helps to protect you from getting into a lengthy one-on-one with a particular audience member, which should be avoided (more on that later).

You should take one question, give one response, and then go on to the next questioner. When in front of a more sophisticated audience or at a press conference, you may find it necessary to permit a follow-up question, but these should also be limited to one. If you announce this rule in advance, you'll find that audiences will happily cooperate. But if you try to announce it halfway through because an audience member won't leave you alone, you'll appear evasive and authoritarian.

Ask Questioners to Identify Themselves

A final Q&A ground rule is to ask audience members to identify themselves as they begin their question. Another move toward democracy? Hardly. You are making use of the fact that people tend to behave themselves when everyone present knows their name. Stripped of his or her anonymity, the most irate questioner is a lot more polite.

You will definitely change the tone of a Q&A session by having each questioner say his or her name (and affiliation if appropriate). You may have to enforce this rule gently at first ("I'm sorry, your name is . . . ?"), but once an audience begins to conform, the results can be dramatic in terms of toning down the more hostile questioners that may be out there.

Set the Tone for Questions: Begin Aggressively

At the beginning of most Q&A sessions there is often a great deal of hesitancy on the part of both speaker and audience in getting started. Audience members tend to sit there wondering what sort of questions are permissible or expected.

An audience may need prompting from you as to what kind of questions or issues are appropriate. For example, do you intend to handle only polite "puff-ball" questions, or get into serious issues? An audience is often unsure about the depth and tone of questioning you expect. At this point you can and should take control by beginning with the phrase, "A question I often get about . . ."

If you intend to deal with serious issues, your self-asked question should be on just such an issue. If you want to steer the questions toward a certain subject, your question should be on that subject.

Be certain to plan and rehearse the opening of the Q&A session, including stating the ground rules and transitioning into your start-up question. These activities will not only set the tone for the Q&A session, but, as the final portion of your speaking appearance, they will also play an important part in determining the impression you make.

Have an Informational Goal or Theme

You may not think you have much to learn from politicians, but communicatively you do. They tend to be very good at sticking with a message and getting it across no matter what the occasion. As you think about the political figures you've heard, you'll realize that they keep returning to and repeating the same themes, such as the economy, the environment, or the plight of the working poor.

Similarly, you should have your own informational goals, which I refer to as *target issues,* for a Q&A session, be it a policy you're trying to implement or a sales goal for your personnel. In advance of the Q&A session, write down and internalize these target issues.

Restrict your target issues to no more than three ideas. If you have too many, your informational goals will be ill defined and therefore will remain unaccomplished. Also, you won't be able to remember many more than three target issues and may be uncertain as to whether you are hitting the most important ones.

Later in this chapter, as a specific format for responding to audience questions is outlined, I'll also show you how to "hit your target issues" by integrating them into your responses whenever possible.

Surefire Techniques for Answering Questions

Please note that the title of this section says nothing about evasive tactics or wriggling your way out of audience questions. The most important rule of effective Q&A management—which applies as much to the media interview, the witness stand, or the job interview as to the post-speech Q&A session—is to *answer the question you were asked.*

This is a simple, basic rule that is routinely violated by speakers in all walks of life. If you take one of the usual alternate paths—such as answering a question other than the one you were asked, trying to joke your way out of it, or becoming inappropriately insulted and refusing to "dignify the question with a response"—the fact remains that you haven't answered the question.

If you don't answer the question you're asked, no matter how artful you consider the evasion, your personal credibility will suffer. Your failure to respond may result in a few perfunctory questions because the audience has decided that any attempt to get a straight answer out of you is so remote a possibility that it isn't even worth the effort. *Answer the question you were asked.*

Now that you've been sufficiently impressed with the need to be honest, you should know about two perceptual steps (which need to occur almost simultaneously) in order for you to respond effectively to most questions.

The first step is to *categorize* or codify the question into one of the usual type that people tend to ask. Doing so will make it easier to formulate a response based on the question type itself.

The second step is to *apply the R.E.S.T. formula,* which will enable you to respond in a focused and organized manner without bringing up additional issues.

Although R.E.S.T. will be discussed fully later in the chapter, rather than keep you in suspense, I'll say right now that R.E.S.T. stands for *Respond, Example, Stop talking,* and *Take the next question.*

I realize that all this stuff about two perceptual steps may sound like quite a mouthful, or even a mindful, but with practice you can carry out these steps easily and with excellent results, both in answering your audience's questions and in accomplishing your informational goals.

Codify the Question

The science of linguistics tells us that language structures or formats are really quite limited. This is especially true when it comes to the types of questions you are likely to be asked in any situation. In fact, there are only about eight basic types.

Being able to "type" the question sets up a response pattern. This question typing, combined with the R.E.S.T. response formula, provides a system to help you through the toughest of Q&A sessions with credibility and authority. Following are the major question types you can expect to hear from the audiences you face.

Yes-or-No Questions

SAMPLE QUESTION: "Senator, will the taxpayers be footing the bill for your upcoming trip to France?"

ANALYSIS: The questioner provides all the information and you only have to fill in the blanks (say yes or no) and, when appropriate, provide an example.

CORRECT RESPONSE: *"Yes, that trip will be paid out of taxpayer funds, but let me tell you what we intend to accomplish . . ."*

INCORRECT RESPONSE: *"As you know, we've been concerned for a long time about building industrial bridges between the people of this region and the good citizens of France. We find that by making trips such as these we can establish contacts that . . ."*

ERRORS TO AVOID

Not giving an immediate yes-or-no response. Remember that the person who asks you the yes-or-no question often knows the answer. By putting off the answer with a defensive statement such as the one contained in the incorrect response, you merely irritate the questioner and give the impression that you would rather not respond.

The tendency in responding to the yes-or-no question, when saying yes or no up front will be seen as bad for your side, is to begin your answer with the reasons why you are about to say something your audience won't like.

The yes-or-no question should be answered immediately and directly, or the evasiveness you display in not getting to the answer right away will be more damaging than the response itself.

But what if the answer to a yes-or-no question isn't yes or no? In such cases, simply say so. In scientific or legal areas, sometimes a simple yes or no can be an oversimplification or truly damaging. At other times it can seem insensitive, even with a qualifier to follow. ("Did you vote against funding for the prenatal clinic?")

With responses structured such as, "While the data point in that direction, a simple yes (or no) in answer to your question wouldn't be accurate," or "Although I did cast that negative vote, you should also know that . . ." the questioner needs to listen to the qualifier in order for the response to make sense.

You should, however, save such responses for situations in which they are really needed. Their continuous use will be ineffective and make you appear evasive.

Caesar-or-God Questions

SAMPLE QUESTION: "As a manager, which policy do you look most favorably on—salary cuts or layoffs?"

ANALYSIS: In James 11:22, a soldier asks Christ which was more important, the laws of God or the laws of the Roman empire. In those days, the wrong answer could be fatal. Even today those who ask you a question that requires you to choose from two alternatives almost never give you a real choice. No matter which one you choose, the questioner or some other audience member will be back with a stinging follow-up question berating your choice.

CORRECT RESPONSE: *"As a matter of fact, I don't like either of those solutions, which is why I've put together a combined early-retirement and attrition program that will help us meet our goals."*

INCORRECT RESPONSE: *"Well, that's not much of a choice, but I'm afraid I'd have to choose the salary reductions as a way to go . . ."*

RESPONSE STRATEGY: Note that in the correct response, the speaker has chosen an alternative rather than one of the choices set forth by the questioner. Therefore the correct response pattern becomes *neither*, followed by an alternative chosen by the speaker, not the audience member.

ERRORS TO AVOID: *Limiting yourself to choices given.* It's a source of constant amazement to me that speakers who might be assertive, self-assured people in so many settings can get completely boxed in by the

Caesar-or-God question, and completely forget about the word *either* or *neither,* or both. Remember that you don't have to be limited in your response to the choices given you by the questioner.

What-If Questions

SAMPLE QUESTION: "What if this division fails to meet its goals for the third quarter?"

ANALYSIS: What-if questions refer to what *might* happen, not to what has *actually* taken place. Unless the parameters described in the question are completely absurd, they are legitimate questions deserving of a response. They are also a good test of how well the speaker has analyzed a situation or issue.

CORRECT RESPONSE: *"First of all, you're raising a hypothetical issue, because our numbers don't indicate that result; but just in case, what we would have to do is reevaluate our staffing needs for the second half of the year and maybe even take some cuts. But once again, you've raised a possibility that I just don't consider realistic."*

INCORRECT RESPONSE: *"If we don't meet our goals, we'll have to look at making some reductions in the sales force, followed by a reevaluation of just how we arrived at those projections."*

RESPONSE STRATEGY: The most essential element in answering the what-if question is to keep in mind that it refers to events that have not taken place. The response should point out the hypothetical nature of the question, at both the beginning and the end, to make sure the audience gets the point.

When the hypothetical situation is just too absurd, or when speculation would be irresponsible, say so and don't respond further.

Particularly in the coverage of military conflicts, when secrecy shrouds much of the activity, reporters will use hypotheticals as a substitute for hard news, as in, "What will happen *if* the conflict subsides?" Commanders have proven very adept about not speculating as to what *might* happen.

ERRORS TO AVOID: *Forgetting that you're dealing with a "what-if" situation.* Often speakers become so involved in placing themselves within a hypothetical scenario that they forget it never happened. This error is compounded by the fact that audiences never listen to every word you say and will join your response "in progress," thereby getting the impression that the layoffs or the nuclear accident you're talking about have actually happened!

The Laundry-List Question

SAMPLE QUESTION: "You and your company have piled up massive losses while you continue to exploit your workers, pollute the environment, and cheat the federal government out of millions of tax dollars, all while your overpaid executives continue to rip off shareholders. What's your comment?"

ANALYSIS: This monster of a question, often heard at annual shareholders' meetings, is not really a question at all but a statement. It's usually made by a person who is either very angry or is intent on disrupting the meeting, or both. The laundry list questioner doesn't really expect a response and should be handled carefully and systematically.

CORRECT RESPONSE: *"You've raised a lot of issues; let me try to respond. On the matter of environmental action, our company has taken a leadership role in placing the latest technology in all our facilities . . ."* (The answer continues at length on the issue you're most comfortable with, followed by a call for another question from another part of the audience.)

INCORRECT RESPONSE: *"You seem very angry. If you can just try and calm down I can begin to address the many issues you have raised. Let me begin with the losses to which you refer. In the past three quarters . . ."* (The speaker continues through the list, asking the help of the questioner if he or she can't remember the entire list.)

RESPONSE STRATEGY

I usually advise answering the question you were asked, but in this case you will note that you haven't been asked a question. Since this audience member wants to make a statement, hurl charges, and disrupt, an answer should not be your priority. Instead, you want to attempt a response and get away from this individual quickly.

Here's what to do and what not to do: When you hear the laundry list, you will be stunned, and your audience will be embarrassed. That means they are on your side, at least temporarily.

Sometimes speakers are so stunned at this moment that they ask for a repetition of the question. This merely brings a longer version, complete with profanity from a now emboldened protester.

In responding, don't refer to the questioner's emotional state or ask for any feedback whatever. All this will bring is something like, "You're damned right I'm angry, you would be too if . . ." and there he or she goes again. Instead, once you hear the list, choose one issue and talk about it for a minute or so. If you get right into it, your embarrassed audience will be relieved that someone rational has taken charge.

At the end of your statement look into a portion of the audience other than where your antagonist is seated and say, "Next question," and pause deliberately.

Usually, in the silence that follows, an easier question will be asked.

If your laundry-list question is still in action, remember those ground rules we set up at the beginning? Now it's time to use them.

If that disruptive questioner is insistent, say, "I said at the beginning, one question per person, and I'm going to stick with that rule. Let's give someone else a chance." Usually an audience will take your cue, and another question will follow.

The important strategy here is to let the audience work for you and against the disrupter, which can happen only if you back off, stick to your ground rules, and use some silence.

In the unlikely event that all these tactics don't solve the problem, invite your antagonist to get together with interested audience members after the meeting. This should mollify the disrupter. By the way, almost no one ever attends those after-meeting meetings.

To summarize, the key strategies for handling the laundry-list questioner are:

1. Respond on a single issue only, and let your response be longer than usual. Choose the issue you're most comfortable with.
2. Avoid going back to the questioner verbally or nonverbally with a glance. If you're looking for approval you won't find it.
3. Ask for the next question from another part of the audience.
4. Stick to your ground rules of one-question-per-person, but avoid an argument.

Practice these steps any time you expect some rough sledding in a question-and-answer setting. They really work, but should be employed smoothly and without hesitation for maximum effect.

ERRORS TO AVOID
Commenting on the emotional state of the questioner or telling him or her to calm down. If you have ever been asked to calm down when you're

angry, you know it can have just the opposite effect. Although the questioner's anger may be a breach of etiquette, it may also be justified.

Asking for repetition of the question. I know how dumb it sounds, but I've actually heard speakers ask a repetition of an angry question, and I have even provoked this response in training seminars from stunned participants. Avoid this attempt to buy time. Only ask for a repetition if you didn't hear the question.

Seeking any kind of feedback from the questioner. Generally a bad idea in Q&A sessions, and especially bad here, it encourages a dialogue with the last person in the room with whom you want to have that dialogue. Maintain control and get away.

Arguing with the questioner. You can't win, so stick to your formula and get to the next questioner as soon as possible.

Legal or Personnel Questions

SAMPLE QUESTIONS: "Don't you think it would be reasonable if your company compensated the Braddock family for their accident on your premises? After all, your PR people invited them on the tour." Or, "Since his drug arrest, do you intend to fire John Freldoon?"

ANALYSIS: Although these questions differ in content, they have a strong common link in that responding to either of them could get you a court appearance, testifying against your own company. Such questions may be asked by the idly curious—or by investigators for potential legal adversaries.

The first question asks for your opinion on compensation in an injury case, clearly a question on a legal matter. Are you *really* qualified to answer? Probably not, but if the question is asked politely and quietly "out of the blue," you might be tempted to respond.

Personnel matters are usually confidential and should be treated as such. As a general rule, don't publicly discuss personnel issues involving individuals.

CORRECT RESPONSE ON LEGAL MATTERS: *"You've asked a legal question, and I'll have to decline to respond at all."*

Or, if more applicable to the situation: *"That matter is currently in litigation and I cannot respond."*

ON PERSONNEL MATTERS: *"It's our policy not to discuss personnel matters publicly, and I'm not going to comment further."*

INCORRECT RESPONSE: *"Sure, as an individual I feel sorry about the accident, and I'd imagine the company will take care of them."*

Or, *"Mr. Freldoon has had quite a substance abuse history, and I think we will be taking some kind of punitive action, termination or otherwise."*

RESPONSE STRATEGY: When you hear words such as "reasonable" or "compensation" coupled with a request for your personal opinion, be careful. Any response other than those presented here could get you into legal difficulty. Similarly, any question involving personnel policy in a corporate setting should be off limits once a name is mentioned.

ERRORS TO AVOID: *Not listening for the words that should trigger the realization that you are being asked a legal question.* Anyone who wants a corporate spokesperson to take a position against the company, particularly for use against the company, needs to be clever about it—and they will be. Be wary of overly polite or meek questioners in such areas.

Personal Questions
SAMPLE QUESTION: "What's your annual salary?" or "We know you're the company expert on environmental issues and get paid to state their

policies, but how do you personally feel about the company's position?"

ANALYSIS: Personal questions from audiences come in two varieties: those that seek information about your personal lifestyle, family background, income, and so forth, and those that seek to determine if you really believe what you're saying or are just going through the motions.

CORRECT RESPONSE: *"My salary? . . . That's a personal matter, and I'm here to discuss company issues. I'll be happy to answer issues inquiries but not personal questions."*

Or, *"Personally, I am happy to say that I've examined the environmental policy studies closely, not just as a spokesperson, but as a resident of this community, and there's absolutely no difference between what I've said today and my personal view."*

INCORRECT RESPONSE: *"Salary . . . I'm afraid that's none of your business."*

Or, on environmental questions (after a long pause), *"I haven't really given it much thought, but I don't think there would be any difference."*

RESPONSE STRATEGY: Audience members often ask personal questions just to test the sincerity level and openness of the speaker; others ask them in an attempt to embarrass you. In responding to personal questions, your reaction can be more important than your answer, in that anger or indignation will lessen the effectiveness of everything else you've said.

Decide in advance how you'll handle such questions and stick with that policy. An audience may not like your refusal to answer personal questions, but they will respect it.

One further note on the issue of salary: If yours is a matter of public record, refusing to discuss it publicly will make you look defensive and needlessly secretive. Also, if you are a senior executive with a salary higher than most, prepare your responses to such questions in advance and be able to justify your compensation level in a calm, nondefensive manner.

The second type of personal question, that which seeks your personal feeling about a policy or issue, seems simple enough on the surface but can actually be a probing and revealing query that, if not handled carefully, can destroy credibility.

The strategy here is to be prepared with a definite position on such a question and to deliver it in the most positive of terms, without hesitation. If there is any hint of doubt on your part, especially if you are slow to respond, the effectiveness of your entire effort will suffer.

Errors to Avoid

In answer to questions that ask about you personally, becoming annoyed with the question or the questioner. This reaction accomplishes nothing. Instead decide on how you'll handle personal questions in advance and politely stick to that policy.

In answer to questions that seek to know more about your personal opinion ("How do you feel personally about . . ."), the biggest errors are as follows:

1. *Being slow or hesitant in responding.* This will be seen as self-doubt even if it isn't.
2. *A bland response lacking in positive language.* Such a response will be read as equivocation and will negatively affect your credibility.

One-to-Ten Questions

Sample Question: "On a scale of one to ten, how would you rate your company's performance as a corporate citizen?"

Analysis: Especially when you have a positive story to tell, this is a tempting question because it enables you to say all the positives you can without even having to think of any sort of elaborate response. All you have to do is blurt out, "Ten!" or the falsely humble, "Nine-and-one-half and climbing!" and move on to your next questioner.

Not so fast. A second look at this question, beyond the momentary elation you feel at having been asked it, reveals that it invites you to oversimplify. Once you play this numbers game, you'll also be obliged to answer "Three" in rating a problem area. Instead, use words, not numbers, as in the sample correct response.

CORRECT RESPONSE: *"Just tacking a number on our performance would be an oversimplification and wouldn't mean much to most of our audience. I'd have to say instead that we're doing an excellent job and hope to continue."*

Or, when the answer might be a very low number, *"If you're referring to the fact that we've had some problems in corporate citizenship, I'll be the first to admit that we could've done better. However I'm not going to oversimplify by just tossing a number at you. Instead, let me tell you about just a couple of the initiatives we've taken to improve things. First of all . . ."*

INCORRECT RESPONSE: *"Ten!"* or *"Three!"* or any numerical response.

RESPONSE STRATEGY: Trade the momentary joy of being able to say "Ten!" in front of an audience for the enhanced credibility of a speaker who refused to oversimplify. This way, if asked to rate a negative area or issue, you're free to respond with words, not numbers.

ERRORS TO AVOID
Numerical or flip answers to a question that invites you to oversimplify. Being unwilling to answer this question on a negative issue if you have already answered it on a positive issue within the same meeting.

Stupid Questions

Those of us involved in coaching speakers and preparing media guests and witnesses, with all of our strategizing, issues analysis, and formulas, sometimes forget that one of the most troublesome and potentially embarrassing questions is the off-the-wall, stupid, or inappropriate one that pops up with surprising frequency in a variety of situations.

It can come from the inebriated caller to a radio or television program or from a member of a club that you are addressing as a guest speaker.

Sometimes a question is stupid or at least out of place because it's obvious to everyone (except the person who asked the question) that you have just answered that very question.

SAMPLE QUESTION: "How will the tax information you have just presented affect my geraniums?"

ANALYSIS: As you struggle to make sense of a question as bizarre as this one, or come to the reluctant conclusion that the question made no sense, an audience's embarrassment turns quickly to curiosity about how you'll handle this delicate situation.

CORRECT RESPONSE: *"I'm afraid I can't give you the information you might need but let's get together later and try and come up with something. Other questions?"*

INCORRECT RESPONSE: *"That's a pretty silly question in light of what we've been talking about. Could you please explain it a bit better? . . . I think I missed something or maybe didn't quite hear you correctly."*

RESPONSE STRATEGY: Your reaction to the questioner and the impression you make on the audience at that moment are more important than the response itself. Exhibiting confusion or embarrassment is certainly appropriate on your part.

Beyond that, your only strategy should be to take the questioner seriously, respond as briefly and sincerely as possible, and get to the next question. The fact that you handled this moment with sensitivity will create a more lasting positive impression than your attempt at a response.

When the question, rather than being bizarre, is merely a repetition of a question you just answered, and it's obvious to all that the questioner wasn't listening, avoid embarrassing the questioner with such phrases as "As I just said . . ." or "If you had been listening . . . ," and simply repeat your prior response.

If you feel the need to let your audience know you are aware of the repetition, you might want to begin your response with a polite, *"I'd be happy to go back to that issue for a moment and let you know that . . ."* It's a lot more subtle than, *"If you had been listening . . . "* or *"As I just said . . ."*

Once again, showing that you are a caring, sensitive communicator is more important than the response. Your audience will appreciate the effort.

ERRORS TO AVOID

Seeking clarification of the bizarre or stupid question. In the case of the bizarre question or questioner, avoid going back to that questioner for clarification or feedback; you'll only make things worse. (See incorrect sample response.) Get to the next question as soon as possible.

Commenting on the quality of the question. Don't comment in any way on the quality of the question, and particularly avoid any humorous remark made at the expense of the questioner. If you try to kid your way out of this moment, you'll come off as slick or snide—either one a very unfavorable impression.

Using the R.E.S.T. Formula to Give Successful Responses

As we begin to take a more detailed look at the R.E.S.T. formula, I'll restate it briefly: Respond, Example, Stop talking, and Take the next question (or go to your Target issue).

Effective communication often means applying behavior we use in conversation to the speaker's podium or media appearance. Responding to audience questions with the randomness and spontaneity that typify conversation, however, can get you into great difficulty in a tough-issues climate. An audience uses the Q&A period as an indicator of the speaker's knowledge, authority, and sensitivity; they will also assess your credibility and skill in communicating under pressure.

The R.E.S.T. formula gives you the following advantages in handling the Q&A session, be it for a media interview or as guest speaker at a meeting of the local Lion's Club:

1. The R.E.S.T. formula, once internalized, enables you to organize your thoughts better, since it provides a definite format for each response.
2. The R.E.S.T. formula permits you to focus on ideas and issues rather than on the structure of your answer, making you more responsive to your audience.
3. The R.E.S.T. formula makes it easier to maintain a consistent length of response from question to question.

One of the key barometers of performance in Q&A is length of response. When a speaker finds a question particularly problematical, he or she either gives an extremely short answer, as if to hope that the questioner and the subject will just go away, or makes an extremely defensive response, as an obvious defensive reaction meant to verbally stomp out any informational brush fires that might flare up in the continued presence of that issue.

Of course, the extremely short answer is perceived as evasive and causes further questions on that issue, whereas the long, multipart response brings up other issues and—you guessed it—even more questions on that dreaded issue.

A consistent length of response helps mask the difficult areas and gives you a chance to handle the Q&A session on a more level playing field.

Step #1: Respond Directly

In one line or a single sentence, give the answer to the question: simply, directly, and free of prior clarification.

SAMPLE QUESTION: "Does your company intend to raise prices over the coming year, and if so, by how much?"

CORRECT RESPONSE: *"Yes, we are looking at a price increase in the coming year, the exact amount being between 3 and 5 percent."* (This response will be added to in Step #2.)

The tendency in this type of question, particularly, is to defend yourself before responding. The result? The audience thinks you are afraid to respond directly or that you are doubtful of your own position.

INCORRECT RESPONSE: *"As you know, our company has had to maintain its competitive position through aggressive pricing strategies, but we also have a responsibility to our employees and our shareholders to remain profitable. Therefore we will be looking at the possibility of raising prices in the coming year."*

This speaker defends the company for the price increase before actually answering the question, with the result that his audience comes to the rapid conclusion that the question has not been effectively answered.

Follow the formula. Step #1 tells you to respond in a simple sentence or phrase, directly or concisely, as in the correct response. Now on to Step #2.

Step #2: Explain with a Single Example

Clarify your response by using a brief, illustrative example. It's important here that you avoid the temptation, especially when the question is easy, or it's on a topic with which you have great familiarity, to give more than one example. In so doing you cause several problems for yourself.

First of all, you are reducing the clarity of your responses. On more than one occasion in teaching the R.E.S.T. formula, as the speaker launched into his or her second example, I've interrupted and said to the audience, "What was the question?"

They seldom remember, because (except for the person who actually asked the question), audiences seldom listen to the entire response. If you keep your responses brief, audiences will be better able to connect questions to your responses, increasing their retention and your impact.

In a media interview, sticking to an example as per the formula will keep the interview in focus and perhaps lessen the need for editing.

Another reason to limit yourself to a single example is to avoid bringing up additional issues. Examples other than the one you planned or the first one that occurred to you are often more tangential to the response. That's why audiences won't easily make the connection between the response and the example, resulting in further questions.

Finally, as I mentioned earlier, it's important to balance the length of your responses. If you spend too much time on an issue, or suddenly deliver a four-second response in a sea of one-minute answers, an audience knows that something is up, and more questions will follow, on an issue you wanted to avoid.

Instead, stick with the formula and limit yourself to a single example. I sometimes encounter some resistance to this part of the formula, as a speaker says to me after delivering a multi-exampled response, " . . . but I was on a roll." I would remind any of you so inclined that things "roll" in only one direction: *downhill.*

Here is an example of the question we started with in the first part of the formula, along with a sample response containing a single example explanation:

SAMPLE QUESTION: "Does your company intend to raise prices over the coming year, and if so, by how much?"

CORRECT RESPONSE (STEPS #1 AND #2 APPLIED): *"Yes, we are looking at a price increase in the coming year, the exact amount being between 3 and 5 percent. You should also know that the increase will be an essential part of our responsibility to both our shareholders and our employees, as well as providing the best possible products for our customers."*

Step #3: Stop Talking

Once you have completed the single example that comprises Step #2, the next thing to do is stop talking.

Including this as a step in a formula might strike you as a bit of instructional overkill, but not remembering to stop, and giving multiple examples, is often a costly error.

We often equate talking with success and silence with failure—to the extent that we sometimes end our phrases with connective words such as "but" or "and" or the verbalized pause ("uh"). This behavior may cover the dreaded silence, but it also causes us to say more.

If you don't learn to end your response at the conclusion of the planned single example, your response ends when you simply run out of ideas or, put less kindly, when you run out of conversational gas. Stick with the R.E.S.T. formula.

Step #4: Take the Next Question (or Go to Your Target Issue)

At Step #4, it's decision time. After you have completed your response you may wish to take the next question. You may, however, want to state your target issue before doing so. It's your decision, but here are some guidelines to help you set the best course of action for Step #4.

Select as many as three target issues for use during a Q&A session. These should be themes that you want the audience to come away with, that you can integrate into your responses.

For example, if I were representing the fictional company in the sample responses regarding a proposed price increase, I might assume that customers would be disturbed by that increase. Therefore one of my target issues would certainly be "concern for the customer." I would try to integrate that theme or target issue into some of my responses by adding it at the end of the response. Following is an example of how the *target issue* concept works.

SAMPLE QUESTION: "Does your company plan to raise prices over the coming year, and if so, by how much?"

CORRECT RESPONSE (WITH TARGET ISSUE): *"Yes, we are looking at a price increase in the coming year, the exact amount being between 3 and 5 percent. You should also know that the increase will be an essential part of our responsibility, to both our shareholders and our employees, and will provide the best possible products for our customers. While I'm on the subject of our customers, once they see the product improvements made possible by the increase, they'll know that they continue to be our number one priority."*

In this response, the speaker made a smooth transition into the target issue, customer concern, after fully responding to the question asked. I would recommend that you try to get to your target issue or issues in about 25 percent, or one in four, of the responses you deliver.

With practice you will be able to integrate your target issue(s) smoothly into your responses, while still answering the questions you are asked.

The final step embodies a couple of simple but important procedures in maintaining the control and flow of the Q&A session.

First, take your next question from someone other than the person who asked the previous question. (Remember your ground rules—one question per person until everyone has had a chance to speak.) This is easier if you focus your eye contact on your entire audience during your response, rather than on the questioner.

Second, don't go back to a questioner for feedback on your response, such as asking, "Does that answer your question?" By doing so you invite a one-on-one exchange that will bore an audience (unless it turns into an argument).

Be careful not to react to the nonverbals of the questioner, which might range from a disgruntled frown to a negative nod. Reacting to such nonverbals will only crystallize the notion that there is dissatisfaction with your response—a sure way to turn the undecided against you.

So once again, Step #4 in the R.E.S.T. formula is either *Take the next question* or *Go to your Target issue*. If you go to the next question, do so decisively, using your ground rules to your advantage.

Using the Anecdotal Response

Once you are thoroughly practiced in applying the R.E.S.T. formula to Q&A sessions, a further step you will want to take is to include anecdotal material as responses to some questions. This essentially means telling your audience a brief story once you have responded to a question, or using the story itself as a response.

Anecdotal responses are effective because, even if their use is planned, their inclusion in a Q&A session is by chance; you happened to get the right question to trigger the story. Audiences appreciate that spontaneity.

Anecdotal responses also personalize the session, as their telling gives an audience an insight into the kind of issues and situations that concern, impress, or touch you in some way, a kind of insight that is not usually gained from the standard exchange of questions and answers.

Let me give you a few cautionary notes about using anecdotal responses.

First of all, keep them brief. If they are more than two minutes long, the audience will remember the story but may forget why you told it.

Second, don't use more than one or two anecdotal responses per half hour of Q&A. If you do, your Q&A session can take on the atmosphere of a gathering around a campfire rather than a briefing by a knowledgeable spokesperson.

Stories about outstanding customer care, employee performance, or perhaps how your company has not just met but exceeded a government safety standard—information that is not generally known to an external or even internal audience—make the best anecdotal responses.

It's been my experience that most companies abound with such stories, which are seldom thought of as sales and public-relations tools. Typically, they are shared at an awards dinner (often being the reason for the award) and thereafter forgotten. Think of one or two and have them ready for your next Q&A session.

Finally, if you use anecdotal responses, make sure they are factually accurate. People tend to remember these stories and may even know people who know the people in your story. If your facts are off or are embellished for dramatic effect, it can be embarrassing.

Stalling for Time

A great deal of this chapter has been spent on getting you to say certain things or at least getting you to organize your response material in certain ways. I'd like to end this chapter by telling you a few things you should never say as you conduct a Q&A session.

The first of these is that worn phrase: "I'm glad you asked me that question." It's usually uttered by a speaker who is desperately trying to buy a little think-time before venturing a response, and no audience ever believes it. If you need a few extra seconds to collect your thoughts, try something less obvious such as, "That's been a serious issue with us for some time, even difficult, but here is the approach we have developed."

An equally overused and never-believed phrase is, "That's a good question!" The fact is that the asker of the most moronic question thinks it was a good question, which is why he or she asked it in the first place. Once again, be honest with your audience, as in, "That's been a tough problem to solve, but here is how we are trying to manage it."

Responding When You Don't Know the Answer

It used to surprise me that even senior executives of major corporations, in a practice Q&A session for a media appearance or for a shareholders' meeting, would nervously say to me, "But what will I tell them if I don't know the answer?"

The illusion of the CEO's omniscience may be good for stock prices, but it's just that: an illusion. Even if you're not the CEO (or even if you are) you're up there handling audience questions because you are recognized as an expert. Remember, however, that *even experts can't know everything, and the most credible ones are willing to admit it.*

If you don't know the answer to a question, simply say so. You might add that you know who does have the information, or even that you should know and will have to get back to the questioner with the information. Don't view the response, "I don't know," as a defeat. If not used more than two or three times in a Q&A session, it can be a refreshing affirmation of your humanity.

Wrapping Up the Question-and-Answer Session

Once you have dealt with the major issues of concern to your audience, you will note that the questions become repetitive or too detailed to maintain the general interest of your audience. It's time to end the session. At this point you should be on the lookout for a positive question, or in a rough-issues climate, a tolerably balanced one.

If it's been a rough session you don't want to give the impression that you're ending things and hightailing it out of town, even if that's what you'd like to do.

End the session by saying you have the time to take a few more questions. Take two, or even as many as four, until you get a friendly or easily answered tough question.

Since audiences tend to remember what you told them last, it's important if at all possible to end the session on a positive note. Therefore you should be direct enough to say something like: "As I said earlier, our time is limited, but I'll be available for a short while to chat with you on an individual basis. Meanwhile, let me leave you with this thought . . ."

At this time go to your *most important target issue* and summarize it once again. Here is a sample summary touching on a target issue:

> *I've covered a lot of ground this evening, but I hope a common theme came through in just about everything I've said, from the tough issues of increasing prices to your well-justified environmental concerns. All of us at U.S. Combinatrix look forward to working with you to make this community a better place in which to live and work. We really care. Thank you.*

A strong closing statement will not only leave your audience with a strong positive final impression of your entire effort, but will also diminish the impact of any missteps you may have made in fielding audience questions.

Watch Your Signal Behaviors

Walk, don't run! Finally, as you leave the stage or meeting, be careful of your nonverbals—that is, don't race out of the room. If you are leaving, say goodbye to those within your gaze and be sure not to make too hasty an exit.

If you are staying to answer individual queries, don't hide in the balcony, but place yourself at a location in the room that is accessible to all those present. Everyone present, even those who leave before you do, will thus have the clear impression that you are communicative and willing to make every effort to tell your story to anyone who'll listen— an extremely important message to send to your audience as they assess your performance.

Summary

People often want to know how to avoid answering tough questions, but my cardinal rule is to always answer the question you are asked. You need to answer it in order to maintain credibility, but there are steps you can take to control the session and the agenda.

First, whenever possible, you should set ground rules before the Q&A session begins. For example, clarify that each person gets one question. (By prohibiting endless follow-ups, you avoid being lured into an impromptu debate.) Maintaining consistency in the length of your responses is another way to stay in charge. If a particular response is overly short or long when compared with your other answers, you risk looking defensive. Using the R.E.S.T. formula (Respond, Example, Stop talking, and Take the next question) is an effective way to balance the length of your response. Some other advice:

- Always enter the Q&A arena with a target issue, or a particular piece of information you want your audience to take away, and state it early and often.
- Learn to recognize various question types (hypothetical, either/or, personal, etc.) in order to respond strategically and successfully.
- If you don't know the answer to a question, say so; used sparingly, "I don't know" is a response with which no one can argue.

Overall, treat the Q&A session as an information-sharing activity rather than a battle. That way, everyone (you as the successful speech-giver, and your audience as a now-smarter group of people) can be a winner.

Quick Review: Handling Tough Questions and Tough Audiences

1. Have an agenda or informational goal for any Q&A session.

2. Set up ground rules for your audience at the beginning of your Q&A session and stick with them.

3. Answer the question each person asks.

4. Keep your responses brief.

5. Decide in advance whether to answer personal questions.

6. Don't buy into the emotional state of the questioner. (If he or she is angry or abusive, don't you get that way.)

7. Don't try to "win" or look at each response as a victory/defeat situation; just answer the question.

8. Avoid saying "That was a good question," or "I'm glad you asked me that." No one believes you.

9. Remember to say "I don't know." Used truthfully and sparingly, it's a bulletproof response.

10. Practice, internalize, and use the R.E.S.T. formula: Respond, Example, Stop talking, Take the next question or go to your Target issue.

CHAPTER SEVEN

Making Effective
Sales Presentations

AT-A-GLANCE SUMMARY

This chapter is about planning, constructing, and delivering a powerful and successful sales presentation. In addition to helping you develop a winning attitude, it provides tactics for handling objections, putting *your* product or service at the head of the pack, and the delicate matter of talking about the competition. You'll also learn the special dynamics of team presentations and how to manage visual aids and sales demonstrations.

Few situations provide so much opportunity for spectacular success or abject failure as the sales presentation. But despite its high-risk nature, many presenters make serious mistakes that are overlooked only because the product or service is so terrific that it's sales-rep proof, or because the competition has done an even worse job of stating its case.

Establishing Your Objective

Before creating a sales presentation, decide what your specific objective is and use every part of your message to work toward that objective.

You can use the speech-building chapter as a guide to structuring your presentation, but do so with a specific objective in mind. The objective becomes your showcase idea, as illustrated in Chapter 4. Objectives of sales presentations include:

1. New business
2. Renewing a prior account

3. Providing product or service updates

4. New employee orientation

The sales presentation that seeks new business is the most crucial and will be emphasized in this chapter.

Every presentation sells, even a seemingly less crucial one in which the purpose is to update an established customer or to train new users of your product. The people in your audience are also gathering impressions about you and your organization. Letting such presentations slide gives the competition a shot they should never get. An "Oh, it's just them" approach to an orientation session may lead the way for an "Oh, it's just you" reaction when you come in to pitch new business.

Sample Objective: Gaining a New Account

This is the traditional success/failure high-pressure situation that most of us equate with the sales presentation—all the agony of public speaking with the added possibility of spectacular failure.

If gaining new business is your objective, everything you do and say in this presentation should be geared toward accomplishing that objective.

Delivering the Presentation

Meet Your Audience before the Presentation

The strategy is based on the fact that audience members are more receptive to speakers they have just met prior to the presentation.

If at all feasible (if the group is less than twenty or so), meet and greet each one as he or she enters the presentation site. Try to remember names and even a few job titles in case you can work them into your presentation. Not only will they know who you are *before* you are introduced, but you will have communicated that you are aggressive, organized, and personable, even *before* your sales presentation has started.

Tell Them Your Goal

If you want a contract signed or an order placed, or if you are there to displace a competitor, say so. Many sales reps are apologetic about selling and are actually afraid to take the confrontational stance of "I want your business today!" They back away from this position because of the potential and immediate chance of rejection it presents.

Instead of saying what they want, such reps usually end their presentation with a quick thank-you and exit with sweaty palms. This way they can get the verdict in a follow-up phone call and face rejection in solitude. Be up-front in stating your objective (getting new business), and you'll have a clear advantage.

Deal with Objections Right Away

Not only must you anticipate objections, but you should handle them as soon as you've stated your objective (introducing the product or product update, making a sale). Getting objections out of the way early leaves you more time to *sell* instead of fending off objections you failed to handle earlier.

Example: "I know some of you here have some problems with Raygor Computers and may think that this is not the system for you. I'm going to give you some facts that will change your mind. Cost was a problem with some of our earlier systems, but that's changed. Sales volume and wide customer acceptance have made it possible for us to . . ."

Be direct and unapologetic in discussing objections and present a clear and concise response to each objection, as in the preceding sample statement. Avoid flip references to product problems, for example, "We really screwed up in pricing the 100 Series!" Be frank but serious: "While the 100 Series may have hit the market at a premium price, that's changed." A flip attitude about problems or a humorous approach will only damage your credibility and make prospects nervous about dealing with you in the event of a future problem.

In deciding which objections to handle, choose the major ones, or those that have the closest application to your prospect. As a general rule, limit objections to three and don't spend too much time discussing them. For example, in a twenty-minute presentation, spend no more than five minutes discussing negatives; otherwise the objections can begin to dominate your presentation.

Discuss Problems Directly

If your product or service has suffered a major setback or received recent negative publicity, don't deal with it by not mentioning the problem at all, much the way an ostrich "avoids" danger by sticking its head in the sand.

Let's say your company has suffered a major warehouse fire that is affecting delivery dates, and everyone present knows it. By not providing some reassurance, or at least a status report, you've communicated at least one of the following messages:

1. You don't know what's going on in your company.
2. You're afraid of tackling tough issues.
3. When the going gets tough, you're the one most likely to leave town.

So don't play ostrich. You have much to gain by dealing effectively with a tough objection or issue, and everything to lose by ignoring it.

As for the order in which you deal with objections, start with the one you are most comfortable discussing, perhaps the one of which you have the most knowledge. In this manner you'll be off to a strong start and be more comfortable once you begin discussing areas with which you have less familiarity.

Selling Your Audience

Once they know who you are and what you want to get done, and after you have dealt with the major objections, it's time to sell.

There are four speech formats that are particularly suited to sales presentations. These are:

1. Problem-Solution
2. Need-Product-Benefit
3. Past-Present-Future
4. Disadvantages-Advantages

The format that works best for you depends on the nature of your product or service and the situation in which it is being sold.

For example, a high-tech product in an industry where innovation is slow to arrive would be a good place to use the historical perspective of the Past-Present-Future format. Show that your product is more evolutionary than revolutionary—an approach likely to be received well in an atmosphere where change is frowned on.

The Problem-Solution format has a wide range of applications, while the Need-Product-Benefit format is easily adaptable to selling a service, rather than a product.

The Problem-Solution Format

In this format you describe a problem of your prospect company in considerable detail. The next step is to present your product or service as the solution to that problem.

One caveat in using the Problem-Solution format is that it requires an intimate knowledge of your prospect's industry and company. Without a high degree of inside knowledge, you are not only likely to make mistakes, but may also seem presumptuous in telling your prospects their own business. The Problem-Solution format works best when you have a long-term relationship with your prospect and a strong knowledge of the company's strengths and problems.

An alternative to the Problem-Solution format is to describe the experience of another client who, by using your product or service, has had good results in solving a problem similar to that of your prospect. If you've chosen a good match or parallel situation, this approach will be effective.

The Need-Product-Benefit Format

This close cousin of the Product-Solution format is a method of tying the product or service to solving a specific prospect problem, resulting in a specific benefit for that prospect. As its name suggests, you begin a sales presentation of this format by describing a need, transition into how what you have to sell will meet that need, and conclude by stressing its benefit to your client.

This format is particularly useful when the product or service being sold is new or has been reengineered to meet a specific client need and thus provide a specific and unique benefit (compared with the competition). Many sales reps feel that this format edges out the Problem-Solution format because you end up talking about how your product or service will benefit the prospect—an excellent way to wrap up a sales presentation as it is more client centered than other formats. Use of the Need-Product-Benefit format ensures that you will end up talking about benefits to the client and almost certainly invite follow-up questions regarding those benefits.

The Past-Present-Future Format

This can be an effective approach if the evolution of a product or advanced product development is a strong selling point. You may wish to skip the historical or "past" part of this format and just go with a brief synopsis of how things are being done, followed by a detailed presentation of your product.

This format is more suited to a prospect who finds change more difficult than do others, or who has used the same systems or methods for a long time. Be careful not to be overly critical of the prospect's current way of doing things. Remember, that prospect has stuck with a competing product or service for a long time because there was, and probably still is, some positive feeling toward your competition.

If you push too hard, you'll only solidify the resistance to change that's already there. On the other hand, if you maintain an approach such as, "What you've been doing may have worked well up to now, but here are some distinct advantages to making a change," you are inserting the wedge you need to make change possible.

The Disadvantages-Advantages Format

If a company is starting up, or opening a new division, or needs a totally new product (all of which can mean you don't have to deal with resistance to change), you may want to employ a Disadvantages-Advantages format.

Here the initial content of your presentation, beyond introducing yourself and your objective, is to be directly critical of the competition. The format is useful in a highly competitive situation where directness and a "just-the-facts" approach are appreciated and are likely to be rewarded by an order.

Some presenters make the mistake of going into too much detail about the competition in the Disadvantages-Advantages format. Balance your presentation so that you spend most of the time talking about *your* product or service. After an initial mention of the competition's name and product, you might merely refer to them as "the competition" or "other products."

One important strategic point to cover is the "disadvantages" side first, so you end up talking about *your* product and its advantages toward the end of your remarks. Remember, those present are more likely to retain what you say *last* than what you say first. It's important to emphasize *your* company, product, and services in all their positive aspects in this final portion of the presentation.

In sales presentations, there are no absolutes about formats. Experimenting with these formats, or even combining them into more lengthy presentations, will lead you to the conclusion that what works best is a matter of what you are most comfortable with, your level of product knowledge, and prospect expectations.

Regardless of the format, emphasizing your product and its advantages and ending up positively and nondefensively should be major goals in structuring your presentation.

Always Answer the Question, "What's So Good about YOUR Product?"

If they are asked this question after the presentation, those present should be in almost total agreement on the answer. This can happen only if you deliberately and emphatically point out the unique selling points (USPs) of your product or service.

Decide what these points are in advance and make them an integral part of the "positives" section of your presentation. That is, if you are using the Problem-Solution format, the solution should be built around the USPs or selling features.

Think of your USPs as *spotlight ideas to your showcase idea* (see Chapter 4). Since we like to think in threes, this is a good number of USPs to include in your presentation. If yours is a complex product or service, you may want to expand to as many as five, but if you include more, you will dilute the impact of your message.

Sales features or USPs should be brief and in headline form. For example: "Calculon maintains the largest support and maintenance staff in the computer business," or "Only Calculon has 1-800-COMPUTE, a 24-hour toll-free hotline for service and information."

Thus, the USPs take on the role of spotlight ideas, all in support of that showcase idea or objective for your presentation.

Concluding Your Sales Presentation

Usually sales presentations end up with a brief Q&A session followed by your closing comments. Your summary statement should contain the following elements:

1. *Thanks for the opportunity of meeting with the prospect.* A brief and sincere thanks will suffice. Don't grovel, as in thanking them for the "privilege" of meeting with them. They won't believe it.
2. *Features summary.* In the briefest headline form, repeat your USPs or spotlight ideas. Be sure to use the *exact* language of your presentation; repetition builds retention.
3. *Repetition of the objective or showcase idea.* Tell them that you'd very much like their business (all customers like hearing that) and then restate the objective with which you began the presentation. If you are seeking an order, say so; if a sales contract, say so.

Close to Win

The point here is to be direct and say that you welcome a positive result. In wrapping up your sales presentation, you are thus linking the positive features of your product with the action you want that prospect to take, an important association to end up on.

Using the Language of Selling

Although presentational language is covered in Chapter 2, the sales presentation requires special consideration and some additional pointers.

Use Client-Centered Language

"It's new." "It's state of the art." "It's at the cutting edge." These phrases are dreadfully overused; they also say nothing client centered.

If you are making a claim about a product, try to do so from a client or "What's in it for me?" (WIFM) perspective: "It's easier to install," "Requires less time," "Increases productivity 15 percent"—these are all WIFM phrases that give the prospect a benefit he or she can readily relate to.

Many salespeople are in the habit of making product-centered claims because such statements require thinking only about the product. Prospect-centered claims require reps to think about the specific customer and link his or her needs directly to the product.

If the claim doesn't mention the customer, re-examine it and see if you can inject some customer-centered or WIFM language.

Be Definite, not Tentative

Think about your reaction if you were sitting in an airliner and the captain said over the intercom, "I hope we'll be landing safely in Cleveland at 7:30 tonight." If you hadn't taken off yet, you'd get off the plane. Why? Because the captain's choice of the phrase "I hope" suggested some doubt about a safe arrival. Such tentative language doesn't belong in the airline cockpit or in the sales presentation.

If you are in the habit of saying, "I think you'll find our products to be . . ." you're being too tentative. Prospects prefer a more positive approach, such as "I know you'll agree that . . ."

Tentative language is a normal part of polite conversation and can easily slip into a sales presentation if you're not careful. If your language choices are tentative rather than positive, that tentativeness will be associated with you and your product. Use definite positive phrases within your presentation and save the "maybe's," "might be's," and "I think so's" for polite conversation.

Some examples of tentative versus more effective positive or definite phrases follow.

TENTATIVE	DEFINITE
It might be possible that	I'll make sure that
I think that	I'm confident that
In the past	My experience tells me
You might want to consider	I know you'll be happy if
I really hope	I'm certain that
If we do business	As our customer, you
We've been pretty happy about	We've been tremendously proud of
Please note that	It's vital to remember
If there's anything I can do	I'm here to help!
We've been pretty fortunate	Business has been phenomenal

Use Superlatives Freely

Your prospect isn't interested in signing up with a firm that has a "pretty good" track record or in buying products that are "among the finest." If you're the best, say so. If you're not, find another reason why buying from you is advantageous and make it a focal point of your presentation.

Don't Apologize for Selling

The sales presentation is no place for apologies. Yet if everyone in the room has a bigger title than yours or the CEO unexpectedly plants himself or herself in the room to hear what you have to say, you might find yourself apologizing for taking up their time.

If you're new to the sales business, you might be both surprised and intimidated by the fact that all these people have gathered to hear from you and may be spending a lot of money based on what you have to say.

Some salespeople deal with their anxiety by apologizing for selling. Such phrases as, "I know your time is valuable so I'll try to keep my remarks brief," or "This is a busy time of year for you, so I'll hurry," indicate that you aren't entirely convinced of the value of your products or service.

Name Your Competition

If you are comparing your product with another, particularly in the Disadvantages-Advantages format, it will be necessary to mention the competition. There was a time, in sales as well as advertising, that direct mention of the competition was taboo. Now, Coke can mention Pepsi, Chrysler can mention Ford, and if Gimbels were still in business, they'd be fair game for Macy's.

Take advantage of this new freedom and mention the competition by name, at least in the early part of your presentation. It shows that you are direct and that you've done your homework, particularly if you know the competition well.

One cautionary note, however: in mentioning the competition, be truthful. Do be afraid to say what they do well and don't exaggerate their flaws, or your prospect will know what you're up to and you'll lose your most valuable sales tool, your personal credibility.

Also remember that a sales presentation should be used to set the stage for your next presentation. Your prospect may already have decided to go with the competition, and although you may not know it at the time, your whole presentation will be moot. In such cases, if you are too caustic in your mention of the competition, you are merely making your prospect edgy and defensive about his or her decision. If you go too far, there won't be any next time for you or your company.

Let Them Look First, Then Touch

You may feel that if you let the customers touch the product (like that certain brand of "squeezably soft" bathroom tissue), they'll be more likely to purchase. Indeed, touching may be a crucial factor. Wait until you have finished the presentation, however, to give out touchables.

Otherwise the person who is doing the touching; the person who just gave up the touchable (who feels he or she let it go too soon and is watching the current toucher); and the person who is about to get the touchable ("He's had it long enough!"); as well as the row of listeners behind this trio ("Why did it start in their row?") are not listening to your presentation.

You should be the focus. Let them know they'll get their chance to examine the product later. The same is true for any kind of handout. Let your audience know the handouts are coming later, but don't give out supplementary material or premiums before or during your presentation. If you fall into this trap, you'll lose the attention of your audience as they pass the material around; they'll then divide their attention between your presentation and the handout.

Using Visual Aids for Maximum Impact

I have included this discussion here because it is in sales presentations that most of us need to use visual aids. Visual aids are just that, a supposed help for your presentation, a visual supplement that should amplify the points you want your audience to remember. Yet, to many speakers, they become an impediment, a distraction that reduces rather than enhances the effectiveness of the presentation.

Tell Before You Show

Your presentation should star *you,* featuring a few visual aids to enhance your major points, not the other way around. *You* should go on first, not a slide or transparency. If any visual aid precedes your presentation, it should be no more than a title slide, which should fade to a blank screen as you begin. Even if you're using that simple but highly effective visual, the flip chart, the contents of the initial page should be covered by *two* blank pages and hidden from view as you begin your remarks. (The audience can see through one page.)

Computer-generated graphics are rapidly replacing slides and transparencies as the visual aid of choice. Some important words of caution are in order if you are working with PowerPoint.™ Don't overuse the wide array of special effects and color choices available. Keep things simple and avoid the overuse of such elements as diamond dissolves or having your images swirl onto the screen. Remember, it's a sales presentation, not a light show!

Don't Stay in the Dark

Dim the light if you must, as you show your slides and transparencies, but stay in a lighted area rather than becoming an anonymous "offstage announcer" for your own presentation. Eye contact, body language, and visual impact of the speaker are all communicative elements that are hidden by darkness; they're all elements that increase the impact of your presentation if you leave the lights on.

Put Up and Shut Up

When you put up a slide or transparency, or as you flip your flip chart to the next page, no one is listening, so don't talk. Instead, give them about five seconds to look at the visual and then tell them what it represents.

After telling them what the visual is, direct them to the portion you want to talk about and wait a few seconds for your audience to find your point of reference. Follow these steps with each visual, and the visuals will work for you. If you don't, you'll be constantly competing with your own visuals, and neither you nor the visuals will win.

Talk to People, not to Slides

One sure way to be overrun by your visuals is to talk to them instead of your audience. Make sure that your eye contact remains with your audience. Know *exactly* what each slide contains, and it will make it easier for you to keep your eye contact where it belongs: on your audience.

As for the visuals themselves, keep them simple and keyed to the text of your talk. Copy should be in headline form, and diagrams should be understandable at a glance. More complicated material such as system diagrams or contract language should be handed out later (which you'll tell your audience.)

The Presentation Should Begin and End with You

At the end of a sales presentation, your audience should have the impression that they just saw and heard a sales presentation with you as the presenter, not a slide show with you as the narrator. This means that your talk ends as it began: projector off, screen blank, and you as the dominant figure.

Organizing Your Visual Aids

Visuals should enhance your presentation; having them out of order or handling them poorly will chop up your presentation or even give it an unanticipated comic tone. Double-check the order of your visuals before *each* presentation and become familiar enough with your projection equipment to keep things running smoothly.

Have a Spare Memory Stick, Projector Bulb, and Extension Cord—and a Spare Presentation

You've probably heard that it's important to carry a spare projector bulb (and it is, just in case). Many projectors come with one placed in the lid for an emergency. Experience and a few awkward moments have caused me to add some other tips.

First, I've seen as many presentations disrupted by the lack of a nearby electrical outlet as I have by the lack of a spare bulb. Carrying even twenty-five feet of extension cord in an unopened package (it takes up very little room this way) might just save your presentation, or might at least help it go the way you planned.

Second, you should be fully capable of smoothly delivering your talk *without visuals,* just in case projection equipment is suddenly unavailable. As an alternative, you might be able to recreate some of your visuals on flip charts—but be ready to go without them.

Your audience, never having seen your presentation or visuals, doesn't really care and won't be all that distracted by the sudden unavailability of the visual end of your presentation, unless you keep saying, "If I only had my slides you'd see that . . ."

Pointers about Pointers

Pointers are just that, pointers—meant to guide your audience to a specific part of a visual. They are not riding crops, conductors' batons, leg scratchers, or walking sticks, just to name a few of the alternate uses I've seen speakers devise over the years. Use the pointer only when you need it, provide the required visual guidance for your audience, and then fold it or otherwise get it out of sight.

If you're using a laser pointer that puts a focused dot of light on the desired part of your visual, don't overdo it. A laser pointer is an excellent tool if used judiciously, but in the hands of the overzealous user who swirls the dot around each point on the slide, it can become a distraction.

Speaking of hands, if the hands holding the laser pointer are just a bit shaky, the light spot dances furiously. Solve this problem by resting the pointer on the podium or on your folded arm.

Using a Product Demonstration

The impact of many sales presentations can be heightened by a demonstration of a product or process in action. Such demonstrations can turn to disaster if you don't take a few precautions. If you're an old hand at these things, you might think you need just one or two run-throughs. You may be right, but you're gambling—an activity that should be reserved for the casino or the track, not the conference room, where you can't afford to lose.

A jewelry wholesaler wanted to impress his prospects with a dramatic demonstration of the impact-resistant crystals on an expensive line of watches. At the presentation, he put the watch on a table and hit it squarely with a hammer. The audience spent the rest of the presentation stifling their laughter as our beleaguered salesman scooped up the parts of the smashed watch. The crystal remained intact.

If a demonstration is to be part of your presentation, go over it at least ten or twenty times and get the bugs out in private. There is really no way to recover from a failed presentation, so don't risk it. Practice!

Making a Successful Team Presentation

If your product or service involves complex technical and/or financial or even legal data, it may be necessary and desirable to make the presentation a team effort, with each member of the team handling the portion of the presentation in which he or she is most expert.

Keep the Presentation Team Small

In planning the team presentation, don't have too large a team—no more than three or four presenters is a good rule of thumb. A larger team will inevitably have varying degrees of presentational skill and experience that will dilute the impact of the message. The mere logistics of more than three or four speakers getting up and down to speak will make things cumbersome.

Going on stage or up to the dais with a large entourage can make it look as if you're so intimidated by the size or importance of the account that you brought along everyone but your receptionist to paper the house.

Instead, use a core team of three or four members with additional support personnel in the room—not as presenters, but as specialists who should be introduced as experts to handle any questions beyond the scope of the presentation team.

Maintain Unity in Your Team

Competition may be healthy among sales force members working solo, but competition among members of a sales presentation team is a formula for failure. For the sake of organizational and communicative clarity, the team should have a leader who will act as chief presenter and introduce the other team members.

All of the team members should support each other! This means that disagreement in front of your audience is to be avoided at all times. Make sure your team knows not to interrupt or correct a team member. A unified team also means not disagreeing with the response of a team member to a question from your audience, certainly not publicly.

A technique to bolster the impression of a harmonious team is to refer to and reinforce each other's remarks deliberately. ("As Linda pointed out in the cost calculations . . .") Of course, use first names only, and once again, *never* publicly contradict or recast each other's remarks.

Rehearse Your Team

A team presentation is generally used in an attempt to capture a substantial account. The best-planned presentation, if not practiced as a team effort, can come off looking as if the team has never played this game before (which might be the case).

Don't just meet, hand out team assignments, and gather at the presentation site. Practice and coordinate such items as:

1. Order of presentation
2. Introductions

3. References to each other's segments (which should
   be planned and included)
4. Distribution of the subjects in the Q&A session
5. Closing summary

If each of these elements is planned and coordinated and the entire presentation is practiced with the entire team present, you will give the appearance of a unified and winning team rather than a bunch of people like Larry, Curly, and . . . who was that other guy?

Summary

What makes selling a tough game is the fact that most sales presentations don't have positive outcomes. If they did, you could become fabulously successful with just a few days' work. Realize that each presentation is a fresh start—a new chance at a positive outcome.

Remember that each new prospect is seeing your presentation for the first time and deserves that "opening-night" level of energy. That level of enthusiasm, along with a truly prospect-centered approach, will mean you have more positive outcomes for more of your sales presentations.

Quick Review:
Making Effective Sales Presentations

1. Know your objective (gaining new business, renewing a prior account, providing informational support), and construct your presentation to meet that objective.
2. Deal with objections right away.
3. Don't play "ostrich" with product problems. Being open about them builds credibility.

4. Don't be ashamed of selling or subtle about the desired outcome.

5. In every presentation, say specifically why your product or service is best.

6. Be prospect centered, not product centered (what's in it for them rather than what's in it for you).

7. Avoid tentative language. Say what will be rather than what might be.

8. In discussing the competition, be direct and factual but avoid cheap shots.

9. If prospects go with another vendor this time, follow up by remaining in touch as you work toward next time.

10. Make yourself the focus of your presentation, not your visuals.

CHAPTER EIGHT

Instant Speeches
Handling Spur-of-the-Moment and Special-Occasion Speeches

AT-A-GLANCE SUMMARY

This chapter is about how to give extemporaneous or spur-of-the-moment speeches and speeches for special occasions such as nominations, awards, ceremonies, toasts, and eulogies—the rhetorical equivalents of fast food—that are minimal, but have just the right ingredients for getting the job done.

The spur-of-the-moment speech is communication's answer to fast food. Like fast-food meals, impromptu speeches may never win any awards, but they do get the job done and quench your ideational appetite, even if only momentarily.

Once you have made a few speeches, your level of terror begins to subside as you realize that you are not only capable of functioning in the public-speaking arena, but you can actually learn to enjoy it. Unfortunately, that state of enjoyment can be extinguished instantly when you hear your name in the same sentence as the phrase " . . . will now say a few words about . . ."

Impromptu or extemporaneous (of the moment) speaking with little or no notice can be made a lot easier if you employ a few simple strategies.

Use Your Mind—Instead of Losing It
The intellectual meltdown suffered by many who are about to give an impromptu speech is both counterproductive and unnecessary.

You may find thoughts suddenly running through your head: "Oh my God! What will I say first?" . . . "What if I go blank?" . . . "I'll tell a joke; no, that might not work," and on and on.

Such rapid fire thinking is totally nonproductive and misdirected. Of course you need something to say, but on the spur of the moment, your tendency is to focus on the exact words to use. You don't need words; you need an idea.

Remember, Language Is Automatic

That's a simple statement—but in gaining the confidence to deliver the impromptu speech successfully, it's an extremely important idea to grasp. When you think about it, you'll realize that almost all the speaking you do is impromptu, without prior planning as to exactly what you'll say.

When you have a reaction to a situation or wish to cause an action by saying something to someone, you do it—no notes, no outlines, just some words generated by an idea or need.

Think about it. If you're waiting to board an airplane and someone walks over and deliberately picks up a piece of your luggage and starts for the exit, you don't stand there and have a debate with yourself about what to say. ("Maybe I'll yell 'Police!' or an expletive . . . No, that would be too strong and this is a public place . . . but then it's an expensive piece of luggage . . .")

The fact is, you react immediately, both verbally and maybe even physically, to get back your luggage. If you did stand around thinking what to say, nothing would happen, nothing, that is, but the loss of your luggage.

Yet, when they are being introduced to "say a few words," most inexperienced speakers will focus on *exactly* what to say and as a result will say very little. The solution to avoiding this mental log jam is in that statement: *language is automatic.*

"If you build it, they will come," said a ghostly voice to an Iowa corn farmer in the film *Field of Dreams*, exhorting him to build a baseball stadium there on the farm. An impromptu talk works much the same way in the presence of an idea. If you have an idea, don't worry about the exact words, they will come.

The point of what I've been saying thus far is to stop focusing on the exact words and focus instead on the exact idea. If I were to stop right here, you might accuse me of having substituted one problem for another. Even if you agree that language is automatic, you may be saying, "So what, unless you have an idea?"

You're quite right, so now let's talk about ways to organize your ideas for the impromptu, spur-of-the-moment speech.

Eight Idea Formats for Building Instant Speeches

If you are given the topic on short notice, an effective approach is to place the topic into one of the formats presented below. As you will discover, an idea format organizes the information for you, and you can flesh out your idea based on your knowledge of the topic. You'll also come to prefer certain of these formats so that their application to a wide range of topics becomes routine, a kind of "formula speech."

Let's say that you're a sales executive at a trade-association meeting and you're suddenly asked to speak on the topic, "Handling Customer Objections." Admittedly, this is not a tough topic for a sales executive, but unless you have a specific direction to go in, you are forced back to the "What will I say?" log jam. Instead, apply one of these formats to the topic and you will have an instant idea as well as a format for your speech.

Format #1: Teach a Lesson

No, I don't mean putting on your professorial robes and launching into an extended dissertation. But what have you learned in dealing with customers that most salespeople either never knew or simply forgot?

What valuable conclusion or insight has your experience brought you? Simply answer either of these questions for your audience and your impromptu speech is done.

Format #2: Define a Term

In this format you're varying the topic to suit your own ideas. Given the topic, "Handling Customer Objections," you might want to define the difference between a real objection and a negotiating ploy that you've heard from customers. Perhaps your audience has largely overlooked a certain customer base out there, and you may wish to redefine "the customer."

Look at your own area of expertise and the topics you are likely to end up talking about. There are usually terms to define or redefine, including, as in the preceding example, terms we use every day. The "Define-a-Term" format works well in that it gives you a chance not only to talk about something you know, but even to talk about the obvious—from a perspective your audience hasn't seen before, you hope.

Here is how the opening of a "Define-a-Term" format would sound for the sample topic "Handling Customer Objection":

> I could talk today about handling customer objections, but before we have the opportunity to handle those objections, we have to know who those customers are. So today I am instead going to offer you an expanded definition of the term "customer," to include some people you haven't previously thought about as potential customers. In the past, we used to define customers as . . ."

Format #3: Describe the Past, Present, and Future

This is a format particularly well suited to the senior spokesperson, and, conversely, less useful to those of you in the earlier stages of a career. If you have been in a field or with an organization long enough to know its history, the Past-Present-Future format is well suited to a wide array of topics.

For example, with our sample topic, "Handling Customer Objections," you could talk about changes in the nature and type of customers, or changes in their objections, in the past, present, or future.

Almost any idea can be put in this format, if you have the background to use it effectively. It's also simple to apply because its sequential nature organizes the talk for you more definitely than most formats do. The only caution is that it can easily become too long for the impromptu talk, which should generally last between three and five minutes.

Format #4: Change the Topic

The formats presented thus far will work well on topics within your own field of interest or expertise. It's possible, however, that you'll be asked to speak on a topic with which you're not totally comfortable. Perhaps you sense that the audience might have more knowledge than you do, or there is a much more pressing issue in need of discussion.

In such cases, you might feel hemmed in by the moment and the pressure to speak on a subject of which you have little knowledge. The speech that follows usually shows it. On the other hand, you don't want to embarrass your host ("I'm sorry, there must be some mistake, because I don't know much about the topic") or yourself ("I'd like to speak about customer objections, but so many of you know so much more than I do . . ."").

Instead, gracefully but directly change the topic to one with which you are more comfortable and proceed with your planned remarks. Here is an example of a deft switching of topics:

> "Handling Customer Objections" is an important subject we all spend a lot of time considering, but because we spend that time, we might begin to lose sight of keying our presentations to the

latest marketing campaign, so today, with your indulgence, I'm going to take a detour into what I'm sure you'll find to be useful information on that marketing plan.

Format #5: State a Problem and Give a Solution

This format is particularly suited to political, community, or personnel management issues, or when combined with the Define-a-Term format, in which you may wish to organize your talk not just by stating a problem but also by defining it and proposing a solution.

Format #6: Agree/Disagree

This is a simple means of doubling the number of options available to you on a topic to be discussed that has pro and con sides.

For example, if you were asked to speak to a consumer group on selecting the best used car, you might instead speak on why purchasing a new car is a better alternative, effectively disagreeing with the assigned topic. If you were asked to speak on the need for continued levels of defense spending by the federal government, you might instead speak on the need for reallocation of resources brought about by world political changes.

Any time you go with an Agree/Disagree format, the rule is diplomacy. In presenting another perspective on an issue, one other than your audience or host expected, the idea is not to say, "I'm right and you're wrong." Rather, the objective, aside from giving you another idea option for this impromptu speech, is to present your thoughts in an "even if we disagree with it, here is a perspective we ought to be familiar with" tone.

The objective is to increase your number of options for speaking material, not to embarrass your host or needlessly turn an audience against you.

Format #7: Base Your Speech on a Quotation

The reason there are literally dozens of books with thousands of quotations is because other people, either through the gift of eloquence or through an accident of timing (they got there first), have said something better than most of us have said it.

Just as many of us have a favorite joke or story, you may have a favorite quotation that is particularly memorable, if not for its humor, then for its appropriateness to an issue or situation. Perhaps its use of language is particularly clever.

If you decide to use the Quotation/Comment format, you will open your remarks with that particular quote and then offer an impromptu commentary. Although this format may seem spontaneous to an audience, it requires that you be prepared to cite a particular quote, usually from memory.

One cautionary note about using a quotation: make sure you do so accurately and that you cite the proper source. Audience members rightly become disturbed by a quotation that's just a little bit off or is attributed to the wrong author, especially an audience that knows your subject area and might have a more than passing acquaintance with the quotation.

Also, if you use a quotation, don't use one that will be obvious to your particular audience, or perhaps stale. I once sat in an audience listening to a speaker try to wow us with his literary acumen by quoting some of the better known words of Charles Dickens. The literary scholar sitting next to me whispered, "If only he had used some good Dickens."

Format #8: Begin with an Interesting Fact

Did you know that there are more radios in the United States than people; or that pasta, that staple of Italian food, originated with the Chinese? or that . . . —well, you get the idea. If you have an unusual statistic or other piece of information that will amaze, or at least momentarily captivate, your audience, it can be a good starting point for your talk.

Using a bit of trivia at the beginning can be a good attention-getter, especially when your audience can relate to it. It can also be a fun way to get started, even if moving to your topic is somewhat of a stretch.

For example, if I were to give a talk on how quickly the public forgets, I might begin my speech by saying, "Can you name me an American President who served in the twentieth century and yet was *never* elected to office?" (The answer is Gerald Ford.)

By making use of these formats, you are far beyond survival and well on your way toward prospering in the impromptu arena.

Preparing for the Impromptu Speech

Now let's talk about developing ideas to plug into those formats. For impromptu speeches that really sparkle, you should be on an almost constant state of alert for information you can use.

Keep a Quotation File

Keep a folder in your computer (or an index card file for older readers) in which you store quotes you might want to use. Clip newspaper articles that contain possibly useful information; when listening to another speaker, be ready to jot down a brief note should an especially quotable utterance occur. Another excellent (and underused) source of speech material is the radio, especially with the increased popularity of talk programming. Much of this programming, whether local or national, is rife with useful information on everything from personal finance to household tips.

In a month of casual information gathering, you will have quite a collection of quotes, stories, and articles that you can apply to a wide array of impromptu speaking situations.

Being ready for the impromptu speech isn't a full-time job, but more a way of thinking. You hardly notice seashells on the beach unless you're collecting seashells. The same is true of ideas for speeches, quotes, and stories. They are all around you, and once you start collecting, it will take surprisingly little time to become a highly proficient impromptu speaker. As I pointed out earlier, once you have the ideas, the words will come.

Relax before You Speak

That is, until you're comfortable at the speaker's podium. The normal tension of an impromptu speaking situation pushes many speakers into the "talking is success, silence is failure" mode, and so they just launch into things immediately and are nervous throughout the talk. Instead, take a moment, establish eye contact with your audience, glance at your notes if necessary, take a breath, and then—and only then—get started.

Consider the Pros and Cons of Using Notes

This is an important decision you'll need to make in accordance with your own comfort level. The general rule in making some "off-the-cuff" remarks is not to use notes; but then the existence of the phrase "off the cuff" originated with British Parliamentary speakers who were said to deliver their orations from notes scrawled hastily on their starched cuffs.

Your comfort level should be the guide to whether you use notes, at least when you're relatively new to the impromptu-speech situation. Eventually you should be able to dispense with notes, secure in the knowledge that your idea will get through. Notes might be useful if you will be reading an involved quotation and it's essential to get it exactly right.

The same rule would apply to a set of statistics whose accurate citing is essential to your message. Think of notes as an even more minimal version of the phrase outline discussed in Chapter 4, a word or two, a format name, but no more.

Think on your feet, not off a card.

Closing Your Speech

Those of us who try to help you, the speaker, pay plenty of attention to getting started, being organized, and not going blank, but we don't say enough about stopping.

This problem is especially apparent in the impromptu speech. You have your idea, you plug in a format, and away you go. But how and when do you stop? Unless you plan your closing, your talk will end with the all-too-familiar shrug followed by an awkward glance in the direction of your host that says, "Get me out of this."

Instead, plan your wrap-up and rehearse it. The key is to use a direct closing phrase such as, "That concludes what I have to say about customer objections. Thank you for inviting me," or, "In ending my remarks, let me leave you with one thought that I hope will be with you well beyond this evening . . ."

You may wish to turn the proceedings back to your host with a line such as, "That wraps up my remarks for now, and in saying goodbye, I give you once more to our gracious host . . ."

The conclusion of the impromptu talk need not be elaborate, but it should be direct, and, most important, it should be there. Otherwise your talk will end either on an abrupt note or on a silence that indicates you have run out of ideas and verbiage.

Practice your conclusion and, especially if you're new to the impromptu-speaking game, learn to rely on one or two stock closers such as the aforementioned. This way you can focus better on delivering the speech, assured that a smooth conclusion is to follow.

Remember, Audiences Are on Your Side

This is a comforting piece of information to bear in mind as you are faced with the prospect of presenting an impromptu talk. The fact is, everyone present is glad that you are the one walking toward the podium instead of him or her.

This "better you than me" attitude doesn't seem all that comforting at first, but audience members know you're speaking on the spur of the moment and therefore don't expect a high degree of fluency of word or thought. Nor are they expecting an extensive or prepared address complete with visuals. Instead, it's just you, an idea or two, some words, and maybe an interesting insight.

Under these circumstances, knowing that an audience wants you to succeed, you might even come to prefer the informality, the conversational style, and the freedom of the impromptu setting.

In summary, to maximize your degree of success in the impromptu talk, internalize the idea that language is largely automatic and that the only real search you need be on is for an idea. Practice using some of the formats covered earlier in this chapter, feeling free to combine them and even invent some of your own.

Finally, get lots of practice. Try an exercise such as turning to the table of contents of a newsmagazine and randomly selecting various topics. Try giving three-minute impromptu speeches on some of these topics, even if some of them seem unrelated to your sphere of knowledge or interest. In words that will undoubtedly be someday attributed to Yogi Berra (I said it, he didn't), it's easy to speak spontaneously, *if you're prepared.*

Preparing Speeches for Special Occasions

A close cousin of the impromptu speech is the special-occasion speech—it pops up on short notice and is often delivered with minimal preparation. This category includes introductions, award presentations and acceptances, nominating speeches, eulogies, and toasts. Following are some guidelines for the various types of special-occasion speeches and some common errors you should avoid.

Presenting Introductions

Introductory speeches, as the name suggests, introduce a speaker to an audience or a new employee or executive to his or her organization.

The major elements in the success and effectiveness of the speech of introduction are clarity of purpose and brevity.

In introducing someone, perhaps the main or featured speaker, *immediately* state the purpose of your remarks to your audience in language as simple and direct as, "It's my role this evening to introduce our featured speaker . . ." followed by the body of the introductory speech.

Within the body of the speech itself, you should include two subject areas: the purpose or topic of the guest speaker's remarks and some biographical information on your guest. Since a speech of introduction should not exceed three minutes in length, biographical items should be limited to those areas that are of some importance to your audience.

Thus if you are introducing the new head of the corporate legal staff, you should be talking more about his or her legal and educational credentials than the person's reputation as a high-school basketball star. Of course, if you're at a sports-awards dinner, you might make just the opposite selection.

When possible, check with the person you're introducing for the inclusion (or exclusion) of items from the introduction. You might also want to examine one of the many *Who's Who* guides for further information on your guest.

Ending the introduction can be accomplished by a call for applause, for example: "I'd like you to join me in welcoming . . ." (you raise your hands to start the applause and turn toward the guest speaker). In a more intimate setting or when applause is not appropriate, a simple "Ladies and Gentlemen, our guest . . . (title and name)," followed by your turning toward the guest, will make it obvious that your introduction has ended.

Errors to Avoid

Excessive length. An introduction, especially if it is for the featured speaker, should not exceed three minutes. If it's much longer, it will lack focus and will not serve your guest; all your audience will remember is its excessive length. If much more needs to be said, it should be done in written form and included in programs for the event or material to be distributed later.

Stealing the limelight. The introduction is for the guest, yet some speakers try to get in on their glory by talking about their close relationship to the person they are introducing. For example, while introducing a former astronaut, saying, "At one point in college I considered joining the space program, but our guest really did!" Leave yourself out of the introduction. The reason you were chosen to do it is that the audience already knows you.

Flowery language. It's an introduction, not a eulogy. Keep your language real and down to earth even in praise. For example, "Christina Bleeker has been nationally recognized as the authority when it comes to knowledge of foreign markets," rather than, "Her performance as a foreign markets analyst has placed Christina Bleeker among the true legends of our civilization, a true oracle in a sea of muted voices . . ."

Such flowery language will do nothing more than embarrass your guest and may even get you a few stifled laughs.

Making Award Presentations

Award-presentation speeches are similar to introductory speeches in that they also serve as an introduction if the audience is not well acquainted with the recipient. In this case, however, the focus shifts from the biographical to specific reasons, accomplishments, or traits for which the award is being given.

If your audience, or the recipient, is not all that aware of the purpose or the history of the award, you should divide your remarks into two portions: the first to explain the award, and the second, a brief biographical sketch of the recipient centering on the accomplishments or traits that culminated in the presentation of the award.

If the audience is familiar with the award, as in a monthly presentation to a sales force, you should focus on the recipient. Three or four minutes should mark the outer boundaries of duration for the presentation speech. Local or organizational custom may dictate a longer presentation, but these suggested guidelines will help keep the focus appropriately on the recipient and the award itself.

ERRORS TO AVOID

"It was a close call!" This is not the time to point out how tough it was for the judges to reach a decision, giving the recipient and the audience the idea that he or she barely scraped through. It's an award, not a qualifying exam, so feel free to praise the recipient.

Don't talk procedure. With all due respect to the accounting profession, one of the low moments for me during the notoriously lengthy telecasts of the Academy Awards is the introduction of the accountants from the firm that certifies or tabulates or does whatever it is they do with the results. This is a classic example of explaining the workings of the jeweled-lever watch movement in answer to the question of what time it is.

Audiences care about the award and who is getting it, not how many ballots, what kind of computer, or how many cigars were smoked in order to arrive at a decision.

Flowery language. Once again this error makes the list because speakers tend to praise in an attempt to be gracious. The award itself should be sufficient praise. Avoid the temptation to speak of living legends, and so forth.

Accepting an Award

Is it just me, or does the line, "I'd like to thank the members of the Academy" immediately come to mind when you hear the phrase "acceptance speech"? Over the years, Hollywood has given us plenty of ideas of what not to do; here is what you *should* be doing as you speak to an audience to accept an award.

Prepare in advance. If you have any idea that you are to receive an award, even if the chances are relatively remote, prepare some remarks and practice them in advance. It's dumb not to prepare, especially since most audiences don't believe that most people who receive an award are truly surprised. All that "Gee, I didn't expect this" stuff comes off as false modesty. Particularly in a corporate setting, an acceptance speech is a magnificent opportunity for self-promotion that you shouldn't overlook.

The acceptance speech should begin by thanking the speaker who presented the award for his or her gracious remarks, followed by mentions of the people by name and title who helped you with this accomplishment. Next thank the judges or whoever was directly responsible for the decision to present you with the award.

A great deal of what happens next is determined by the traditions and rules of the award-givers. For example, if yours is one of a series of awards, you may have time only for the aforementioned thank you. If yours is the major presentation of the gathering, you should describe (from your perspective) the genesis and history of the accomplishment that led to the award. Finally, you should inform your audience of what the award means to you personally, perhaps how it will change or affect your future work.

Speech contents such as describing the award-related accomplishment(s) or what an award means to you personally are interesting to audiences and are best delivered when prepared in advance. So if at all possible, prepare and practice the acceptance speech; use minimal but legible notes to guide you; and enjoy the moment.

ERRORS TO AVOID

Being unprepared. As I stated earlier, people don't believe your surprise, even when it's genuine. At best you'll look disorganized.

Being shocked. If you receive an award, don't demean yourself by saying you didn't deserve it or expressing your disbelief that the award went to you. If there was any competition for the award, there will be those in the audience who will agree that you didn't deserve it, and you'll just be confirming their feelings.

Dragging out your soapbox. I said before that the Academy Award telecast has given us ample instruction on what not to do in awards ceremonies. Nowhere is this more true than when some ungrateful clown decides to use the award forum to bemoan the disappearance of the passenger pigeon or demand justice for those who are alleged to have captured Amelia Earhart.

If you have a cause to espouse, don't embarrass everyone present by launching into it at this moment. You'll do little to help your cause, and you'll end up making your remarks to an instantly hostile audience.

Making Nomination Speeches

Nomination speeches are usually very planned events, and the fact that you have been asked to give one means, or at least your audience will assume, that you are highly supportive of the person whose name you are placing in nomination. Therefore, your personal commitment to the candidate should be expressed in the speech. If absent, it could be taken as a signal that your remarks are less than sincere. If you know the nominee, say so, stating the basis and character of that relationship in a manner that supports his or her candidacy.

The nomination speech should highlight the accomplishments and positive characteristics of the nominee as they relate to fulfilling the demands of the position being sought. In addition, if a single overriding trait makes the candidate deserving of the nomination, be it heroism, leadership ability, prominence in his or her field, a proven track record, or any such defining characteristic, you may want to build the speech around that particular trait, making it a recurring theme as you describe the office being sought.

If a negative issue will be brought up during the nomination speech of an opposing candidate—for example, if your nominee has been in his or her field a short time—face that issue briefly but squarely, and do so just before the halfway mark in your speech. Audiences tend to remember best what they hear last and will retain more of your positive points.

Here is an example of how a possible negative might be handled:

Before being completely overtaken with my deep enthusiasm for this candidate, let me say that I know some of you might feel that Art Crane should be with us a while longer before seeking this office. I'd invite any of you to take a close, detailed look at the record of *exactly* what Art has accomplished since joining us. If that record is measured, as it should be, in achievement and ability, Art Crane will *most definitely* be your nominee.

Note that while dealing with a potential negative, the language is positive, nondefensive, and enthusiastic. If this were a three-minute speech, you would not spend more than thirty seconds dealing with negative issues.

A good rule of thumb for the best length for nomination speeches is that they not exceed 20 percent of the length of the acceptance speech, with a three-minute length being the minimum.

ERRORS TO AVOID
Outshining the nominee. Know the skills level of the nominee and remain compatible with it. If your reputation is that of a master orator, you might consider leaving some of your rhetorical armaments at the door. Otherwise you'll risk the politically embarrassing predicament of finding that the audience prefers the nominator to the nominee.

Exaggeration. Yes, we know you like the candidate, and we're glad you said so, but that "born in a log cabin that he built with his bare hands" is the stuff of comedic caricature and should not in any way slip into nomination speeches.

Also remember to keep your facts straight. The opposition will be listening, and an error of fact could create a decidedly disruptive side issue.

Giving Eulogies

A eulogy, or speech of tribute to a deceased friend or colleague, is a type of speech many senior managers and executives end up having to deliver at some point during their careers. Such farewells are speeches of tribute, a remembrance of the positive and endearing aspects of that colleague, and definitely a time to minimize if not ignore any negatives.

In many ways the eulogy parallels the nomination speech in that it is one of tribute, minus the obligatory call for a vote. It is also time to define and characterize your relationship with the deceased in a caring tone.

Unlike the nomination speech, since there is no election in the balance and no strategy other than the creation of a fond memory, a good framework for the eulogy is to define the most noteworthy and endearing trait of the deceased and then tell a story of an encounter you had with the deceased that defined that characteristic.

If there is a glaring negative, it's best left unmentioned, but if you must include it, do so with the greatest delicacy. A good strategy here is to point out the good that was done for so many, despite what may have been perceived as a negative. Even if you are talking about the company taskmaster, or someone who was known around the office as the "bean counter from hell," remember that reverence for the deceased and sympathy for his or her family rules in such situations.

If, in your judgment, the atmosphere and the subject of your eulogy invite the mention of a negative, be certain to balance it with a positive in the same sentence. For example, "There isn't one of you here today who escaped what some considered 'the wrath of Fred' as he reviewed your expense accounts, but there is also no one here who would argue that Fred's dedication and concern for our well-being and success always exceeded his decibel level."

Whenever possible, consult the family of the deceased in planning your remarks. Perhaps there is a trait or an event that they would like to have highlighted. The length of a eulogy is usually proportionate to the depth and length of your relationship with the deceased, but it would be wise to make your judgment out of consideration for those present.

You should also be attentive to the overall length of the services, as well as the wishes of the family. When a series of eulogists will speak, limiting your remarks to no more than five minutes is a good rule of thumb. If you are the major eulogist, a speech of five to ten minutes is more appropriate.

ERRORS TO AVOID
Excessive sentimentality. Your communicative goal should be to create a fond moment for those paying final tribute to the deceased, not to depress those gathered with tearful good-byes and sentences that begin with phrases such as, "Never again will we . . ."

Humor. Be it a case of denial in helping you deal with your own grief or a misguided attempt to honor the wishes of the deceased who, let's say, was a firm believer in irreverence, the reality and terrible finality of such an event makes humor of any kind a strict taboo for most of us. So let solemnity be the communicative order of the day.

Brutal candor. Eulogies are meant to instill fond memories, not to deliver a "tell it like it is" biography. As I pointed out earlier, if there is a glaring negative to be dealt with, do so ever so briefly, balancing your remark with a positive. If there are several negatives, you are better off leaving them to be dealt with by a higher authority.

Offering Toasts

Drink (alcoholic or nonalcoholic) has long been the preferred conversational lubricant in many business and social settings. In the more formal or important of these occasions, you may be asked to present that short but potentially tricky speech known as the toast. The toast is an ancient ritual said to have originated in England shortly after the time of Christ.[2] In ancient Rome, men were expected to toast their mistress with as many glasses of wine as there were letters in her name.

Happily, things have toned down quite a bit, and this ritual is much less complicated today than it was in Roman times. In a business setting, however, the toast can be a tricky assignment because it requires the best of wit, brilliance, and memorability, all in an interval brief enough to prevent participants' arms from getting tired as they raise their glasses skyward.

It should be said, however, that the challenge becomes a bit less daunting because the memory of a less than sterling performance may be somewhat dimmed by the libation that immediately follows.

The keys to successful toasts, as to so many speech situations, lie in a keen knowledge of the audience: what their tastes are in humor—George Bernard Shaw or George Carlin—their tolerance or fondness for irreverence, the high-mindedness or low-mindedness of their wit.

Toasts have a better chance of being remembered if they are not only suited to your audience but also chosen with the occasion in mind. For a complete selection of toasts, I'd recommend the Paul Dickson book cited earlier, or the many Internet sources of toasts. Otherwise you might want to look at one of the many books of quotations for ideas. Meanwhile, to help you get started, here are a few toasts of the all-purpose variety:

---

2. Paul Dickson, *Toasts: Over 1,500 of the Best Toasts, Sentiments, Blessings, and Graces,* revised ed. (New York, Crown Publishers, 1991).

"May life bring you an abundance of friendship, love, accomplishment, and good health in amounts that exceed your grandest expectations."

"L'chaim—to life."

"You have deserved high commendation, true applause, and love." (Shakespeare, *As You Like It*, Act I)

"May the very best days and happenings of your past pale in comparison with the best days of your future."

"May the road rise to meet you, the wind always be at your back, the sun shine warm upon your face, the rain fall soft upon your fields and until we meet again, may God hold you in the palm of his hand." (Traditional Irish toast)

"To our very best friends, who know of our faults and love us in spite of them!"

ERRORS TO AVOID

Long toasts. Especially if a series of toasts is given, more than three sentences is the kiss of death. Keep it short and make it memorable.

Offensive toasts. Even if you're in a crowd where ribaldry and profanity are not taboo, they are still unnecessary. Playing "can you top this" with vulgarity is the worst kind of pandering to your audience and a losing game for any speaker. Besides, you would be amazed at the ability of people to be offended by what you might consider the blandest of humorous remarks, even when you aren't trying to be vulgar.

If you are in a setting where you are regularly called on to perform such ritual communication, you will find that you soon develop a repertoire of favorite toasts that with minor adjustment are largely suitable to any occasion.

Summary

Instant speeches are the fast food of oratory; like fast food, they work well when the time for both preparation and consumption is limited. Begin with an idea and remember that language will occur automatically. Practice using some of the formats and techniques included in this chapter; and when you are finished, stop talking!

Quick Review:
Spur-of-the-Moment and Special-Occasion Speeches

1. Remember, language is automatic, so seek an idea and the words will happen.

2. Have a few idea formats in mind, for example, teaching a lesson or defining a term.

3. Collect interesting quotes and trivia; they make excellent starting points for spur-of-the-moment speeches.

4. Pause as you start, to collect your thoughts and settle your audience.

5. Keep notes to a minimum, no more than a phrase or two.

6. Remember that audiences are supportive of the impromptu speaker (they're glad you and not they are up there).

7. During introductions, talk about your subject, not yourself.

8. In giving an award, the recipient is the star, so keep your remarks minimal.

9. In accepting an award, thank the people and clear out; stay off your soapbox and avoid false modesty.

10. In delivering a eulogy, err in the direction of excessive praise over excessive candor.

PART THREE

SUREFIRE STRATEGIES
FOR SPECIAL SITUATIONS

CHAPTER NINE

The Job Interview

AT-A-GLANCE SUMMARY

This chapter presents tactics to help you succeed in the job interview. It looks at many of the questions you will be asked, as well as the reasons behind them, and gives you specific tactical information on how to deliver the best responses.

Other topics covered include preparing for the interview, having the right attitude, and avoiding the errors job candidates commonly make.

Whether it's one of your first attempts or you've played the job interview game before, it's not a game that changes all that much from entry level to executive position. Any job interview is a highly structured encounter in which you are questioned in a formal atmosphere, speaking mostly when spoken to, in response to a set of largely predictable questions. Some of the questions are strictly informational and relevant, others trivial and maybe even illegal. Some will be asked in an attempt to trip you up or to see how you react to stress.

Interviews are stressful for most of us because we control neither the content nor the outcome. Our lack of control of the situation is underlined by the fact that it is one of the few conversations we have in our adult life in which we are literally dismissed from the room at its conclusion.

The pressure is intensified if you have been through a series of interviews in which the outcome has not been positive. In such cases, you are probably aware that certain errors can be "fatal," and a sense of desperation may creep into your performance, making matters worse.

If you are beginning to feel that the deck is stacked against you in the interview, it is. This chapter will show you steps you can take to improve your odds and even turn them in your favor.

Avoid the Usual Pre-interview Blunders

Blunder #1: Gaps and Glitches in Your Résumé

Make sure your résumé adds up chronologically. Job candidates often omit a negative career experience or fail to account for some time in which they "stepped out" of the workplace, leaving a gap in the résumé that they don't expect people to notice. I've interviewed people with such gaps and have yet to see one who wasn't surprised that anyone noticed.

Have Dates in Your Résumé

Some résumés avoid dates altogether, or merely list a starting year for a job, with no reference to how long the position was held. Your reasons for such vagueness might be to mask your age or to blur the amount of experience or time spent in a series of positions. Such evasiveness only raises more questions and gives the impression that you have something to hide. Even if such gaps and glitches in your résumé don't stop the prospective employer from interviewing you at all, the interviewer will have to start off by clarifying your omissions or mistakes and you will begin the interview on the defensive—a very poor starting posture.

Blunder #2: Your Objectives Statement Is Not Compatible with the Position Being Sought

Many résumés contain an objectives statement such as: "To obtain an executive-level position in the public-relations field that will enable me to use my media-management experience and high level of interpersonal skills for the benefit of client companies." This statement is fine if you are seeking a position in the public-relations field, but it will not serve you well in aerospace manufacturing.

Employers like to feel they are unique and that you want to work only for them. Job seekers, especially those engaged in an extensive search, can seem especially lazy from an employer's perspective if their objectives statement has a generic ring to it. In this age of computers and word processors, there is no reason why your résumé shouldn't be tailored for a particular position or career area, especially when it comes to the objectives statement.

Blunder #3: I Thought You Said East Broadway!

Woody Allen once said that 80% of success is showing up. You know how to dress and how to get there on time, but do you know *exactly* where the interview is going to be held? You may go to great lengths to prepare for an interview and then undo all your good work by being in the wrong place at the appointed time.

Double-check the location, and make sure you have the correct address. This seems like a minor detail, but Woody Allen was right. If you don't show up, or show up late because you've been stuck in crosstown traffic (and look it!), it can really steal the thunder from all those remarks you had planned to make about yourself as being terrific at handling small details.

Blunder #4: Being Underprepared

Just who are these people, anyhow? What are the objectives of the company? What does it produce? How many divisions are there? How is the organization doing—last year, or this quarter? What are the major issues facing management? Just who is that management?

Answers to all these questions are contained in the company's annual report. Most interview candidates read it in the reception area just before the interview. You should read it well in advance of your interview. (Note: Annual reports may be obtained from the shareholder relations office or public affairs departments in publicly held corporations.)

Even if you don't understand all the financial data, you will come away with a good sense of the company's issues, climate, and future outlook. Just in case your interviewer has the same last name as the CEO (chief executive officer), by asking if they are related you will have made it obvious that you have done your homework.

A further source of information not too often used by job seekers is the employee newsletter or bulletin. Try to learn the level of employee public service, recent promotions, and major internal issues from an employee perspective. It is a mistake to submit to a job interview without having read this material in advance. If you have a sense of the major issues facing a company, its new programs or products, or even the names of its senior executives or board members (one of whom might be present at your interview), you will easily differentiate yourself from other candidates. You will use such knowledge in your responses to interview questions and will leave the impression that you are organized and interested in the interviewers and their company.

Communicate a Winning Attitude

Know Your Strengths and Be Sure You Communicate Them

An essential part of communicating a winning attitude is telling your interviewer what you like about yourself—the positive traits that will make you an asset to that employer. Decide *in advance* which positive traits about you, your experience, or your background you want to highlight in the interview.

Pick three or certainly no more than four items about yourself that are most compatible with that position or company. Write these traits down and internalize them. Practice including these traits in your responses.

Avoid the Competition

Don't show up too early for your interview. They'll think you have nothing better to do with your life, which may be true, but it's not an impression you want to convey.

Another disadvantage of an early arrival is that you will see and sometimes talk with other candidates. These conversations never provide an advantage. The other candidate may say something like, "You mean you don't have a law degree and you're still bothering to go through with the interview?" or "I hear the whole thing is rigged and none of us has a chance." Such discouraging souls may have the wrong information, but they can still throw you off your game plan by causing you to compete with them.

Show up for the interview about five minutes before you are scheduled, and you will not only minimize the anxiety-provoking waiting time, but you'll also avoid the competition and be better able to concentrate on the task at hand.

Make a Commanding Entrance

As you enter the interview area, be aggressive enough to shake hands with your interviewer, or each member of the interviewing committee if feasible.

In a formal committee interview setting, you can expect an introduction by the committee leader, followed by some introductory remarks of your own.

Let Them Know You Want the Job

To armor themselves against what they perceive as a stacked deck, some interviewees steep themselves in an attitude of resentment toward the interviewer. This is conveyed by behavior that says, "I really don't need this job," or "I may even be too good, but I'll consider taking it."

For example, I once interviewed an individual who was, at least on paper, the most highly qualified candidate for the position. Perhaps it was those strong qualifications, as well as the attitudinal factors mentioned earlier, that prompted this poor soul to open the interview with: "Before we get started, let me tell you how I define this job and what I will and will not be doing if I get it." While I vividly remember this opening statement, I remember little else of this encounter, because for me, it ended with those unfortunate words.

Don't act as if you don't want the job, because you just might succeed in convincing your interviewer to buy your act! Actually wanting the job and being willing to say so is an important part of winning at the interview game.

The Interview Begins

After the introduction and the ritual comments about such items as weather, your trip to the interview site, and so forth—avoid stories here, no one really cares—the interview will begin, with the first substantive question.

The interview has a specific purpose (to see if you're suitable for the job), and you have a specific objective (to seem more than suitable for the job). There is no one perfect answer to every question, nor can every possible question be anticipated. Most of the questions are quite predictable, however, and, with practice, can be handled effectively.

The following section contains a series of interview questions and variations you can expect to encounter, along with analysis, advice, and sample responses for the most difficult or crucial questions. Remember always to respond with your own words and use the sample responses only as a guide.

Handling the First Question

SAMPLE QUESTION: "Tell me about yourself."

ANALYSIS: Not really a question but a pleasantly delivered command, this common interview opener seeks to look beyond your résumé and get a picture of "the real you." Unfortunately, many candidates stumble here because they fail to anticipate the question and therefore have difficulty deciding what to include and what to leave out.

You will want to demonstrate that you are career focused. Therefore you will want to center your response on a recent job or educational experience. Personal items such as marital status, hobbies, birthplace, and so on should be mentioned briefly and only in positive terms.

SAMPLE RESPONSE: *"First of all, I'd like to thank you for the opportunity for this interview. About myself, I'm a recent graduate of Regency College with a degree in marketing. At Regency, I worked at the college radio station and developed a real interest in your business. I've had two successful jobs in the record industry, as a talent coordinator and a distribution manager, and I'm looking to build on that success. On the personal side, I grew up in Los Angeles, I'm single, and I have lived here all my life. My hobbies are sailing and collecting big band records. Does that answer your question?"*

ERRORS TO AVOID: *Being too personal or too negative.* Since most interview candidates fail to anticipate this question, the tendency is to make a snap decision about what to include and just ramble on for a minute or so. This is how such items as a nasty divorce or your mother's diabetic condition end up in a response that makes the interviewer as uncomfortable as you are.

Keep your response oriented to business and credentials, with only minimal personal information. If the interviewer wants a more personal response, he or she will ask.

Personal Questions

Any potential employer is going to be making a substantial investment in you, and you will be expected to be asset. Part of that equation means fitting in as a member of the employer's team. Therefore you can expect a number of personal questions that seek to know more about the person behind the résumé. For example:

SAMPLE QUESTION: "Why should we hire you?"

ANALYSIS: This question is really an invitation to market yourself. I have already suggested that prior to the interview you develop an agenda that consists of three or four positive points about yourself that you want to mention. If you haven't used any of these positives yet, here is the place to start.

SAMPLE RESPONSE: *"As I've said earlier, I have a proven track record and a long-term interest in this business, which isn't just professional but personal. At the risk of sounding immodest, I've gotten real results for anyone I've worked with, and I'd very much like the opportunity to make that kind of commitment to you. I know I have the ability and am certainly among the best qualified."*

ERRORS TO AVOID: *Arrogance,* including the mistaken notion that no one else can possibly do the job or that the organization cannot survive without you. It can.

SAMPLE QUESTION: "How does your experience compare with that of most people interested in this position?"

ANALYSIS: This question is really another way of finding out what you think of your own ability. Also, if your résumé contains an obvious deficit, such as lack of a required credential or particular type of experience, this is the time to deal with it in a positive way.

SAMPLE RESPONSE: *"I'm probably among the few with such wide-ranging experience over a relatively short period. In fact, just in case you're concerned because I've worked in the industry for fewer years than some of the other people you'll be talking with, I should let you know that I didn't include any of my apprentice time in college in my résumé. I limited the résumé to paid experience, but those internships should certainly be counted. So, to summarize, I believe that my overall qualifications can definitely be characterized as second to none."*

ERRORS TO AVOID: *Knocking the competition.* Be gracious here and don't belittle candidates with experience or credentials that differ from yours.

SAMPLE QUESTIONS: "What are your special qualifications?" or "What particular trait makes you uniquely qualified to handle this job?"

ANALYSIS: This is a question that, because of its simplicity and the reluctance of many of us to engage in blatant self-promotion (even if requested), can be difficult if your response isn't planned. It's also another chance to accomplish your agenda and reinforce one of your positive traits.

SAMPLE RESPONSE: *"I'd have to say that my industry knowledge sets me apart from most of the people you'll be seeing. I've spent years on a consistent career track that's given me the opportunity to view this field from many perspectives, and I believe that makes me really effective."*

ERRORS TO AVOID: *Not having a planned response.* If you don't plan your answer to this often-asked question, your response can lack focus.

SAMPLE QUESTIONS: "Why did you leave your last job?" or "Why are you looking to leave your present job?"

ANALYSIS: On the surface this question seeks the information it asks. But it is also asking if you are running from a problem, or whether there is some pattern of instability shown in your occupational behavior.

SAMPLE RESPONSE: *"For me, changing jobs is a matter of seeking career growth and advancement. As you might know, the Sell-Quest chain has had its problems over the last few quarters and the outlook was not good. I needed room and opportunity for advancement that just wasn't there, and so I decided to make a change."*

ERRORS TO AVOID: *Excessive negativity or lack of candor.* Your answer should not be an attack on a prior or present employer, no matter how justified or appropriate you might find it.

SAMPLE QUESTION: "What are your personal goals?"

ANALYSIS: This open-ended question can provide a wealth of information in such areas as how driven or ambitious you might be, how important family life is in relation to your career, and how willing you are to talk about yourself. This is a question that cannot be effectively answered without prior planning and thought. Your response may even give the interviewer an indication of your attention to detail as well as your analytical skills, as indicated by the thoughtfulness of your response.

SAMPLE RESPONSE: *"Accomplishment and the rewards that go with it. I am referring not just to the monetary rewards but the deep sense of personal satisfaction that comes from looking back on a career and realizing that you've made a real difference, not just for yourself, but for your colleagues as well."*

ERRORS TO AVOID
Failure to anticipate the question. This is a question that requires prior thought or the result will be a vague or rambling answer that will

create doubts about everything from your sincerity to your analytical ability. Plan ahead!

Humorous responses. Some respondents use humor in an attempt to mask their ability to deliver a substantive response. So avoid the "I want your job" sort of response. An attempt at humor here will fail, especially if you do want your interviewer's job.

Other Personal Questions You Can Expect

SAMPLE QUESTIONS: "Do you consider yourself a team player?" "What do you like best about yourself?" "What do you like least?"

ANALYSIS: In responding to any of these personal questions, you already know enough to present your best side when they ask for a positive. In discussing what you like least about yourself, however, keep your response brief and try to present a negative they'll like, such as overattention to detail or even a small degree of workaholism.

Loyalty Questions

From entry level all the way to the executive suite, almost every member of a company gains access to confidential information. A good indicator of your level of loyalty and integrity is the terms in which you discuss your former employer or the one you are about to leave. The assumption is that if you are about to bad-mouth them, you might do it to this potential employer in the future.

SAMPLE QUESTION: "I hear your former company was a really crummy outfit—what do you think?"

ANALYSIS: This seems like a straightforward and simple question, but it's actually a potential trap. If you left your last job under unpleasant circumstances or harbor some negative feelings toward that employer, you'll be tempted to pay them back with a few nasty comments. Don't do it. You'll come off as spiteful and untrustworthy, even if your remarks are accurate.

In contrast, by declining to comment on problems at another company, you'll communicate an ability to be loyal, even to a former employer, and you'll gain the trust of your interviewer(s). Of course, if there are large issues that are public knowledge, you may be asked to comment, but stick to what everyone has read in the newspapers and decline to provide any "inside information."

SAMPLE RESPONSE: *"I really don't agree with your terminology. As you know, Sell-Quest had some problems and was reorganizing its marketing department, but they were a decent employer and even wanted me to stay on longer."*

ERRORS TO AVOID: *Being too quick to criticize a former or present employer.* The interviewer will assume you'll be doing it to them in the near future. Also avoid revealing confidential information, even if you think you're showing your worth by doing so. Nobody likes a traitor, much less hires one.

Other Loyalty Questions

SAMPLE QUESTIONS: "Tell me the inside story on your former boss."
"Is the drug problem at that company as bad as I've heard?"
"Are you glad to be getting out of that place?"

ERRORS TO AVOID

Disloyalty. Loyalty questions present the occasion to show your degree of loyalty and personal integrity. Don't use these questions as an opportunity to take shots at companies or individuals in your past, no matter how legitimate your gripes may be. If pressed, discuss only matters that are public information and then only briefly and in polite terms.

Revealing confidential information. Avoid going "off the record" or discussing trade secrets. If you are willing to betray a past employer, they'll assume you'll be willing to do the same to them in the future.

Stress Questions

Grace under pressure is often a key ingredient in any job situation, especially those that involve problem-solving with clients and dealing with difficult people and situations in the workplace. In a competitive environment or in the sales world, you are also likely to face rejection or negative outcomes along the way. By asking stress questions, or questions that might even ask you to discuss a negative aspect of your own performance, your interviewer is seeing how you react when the going gets rough.

SAMPLE QUESTION: "Tell us about your worst on-the-job mistake or error in judgment."

ANALYSIS: This is the job interview equivalent of the question: "When did you stop beating your wife?" It clearly asks for a negative, but it is also a test of your humanity and honesty. Anticipate this question and be prepared to talk about a negative. The key here is to discuss an error that was not overwhelmingly negative or catastrophic—one that shows you're human and even willing to admit it. If you can, as in the sample response, try to discuss a negative you were able to turn into a positive. Also, after you've clearly admitted a mistake, politely and nondefensively redirect your response to a positive.

SAMPLE RESPONSE: *"I once ordered a month's supply of stationery with our company's old address, but after some initial embarrassment, we ended up giving it to charity and even getting a tax deduction in the bargain. Obviously I'd rather focus on what I did well at Fereton Industries, which included running a department for three years that became known for its high morale and even higher productivity."*

Other Stress Questions

SAMPLE QUESTIONS: "Why should we hire anyone who admits to making mistakes?"

"Why have you had so many jobs?"

"Why should we hire a new graduate like you when we can get an 'old pro' for similar money?"

or "Why should we hire an 'old pro' when we can get a new graduate with fresh ideas for less money?"

ERRORS TO AVOID: *Angry or defensive responses, even if the question is seeking them. Admitting errors but then blaming others* or the equally fatal, *"I never make mistakes."* Also resist the temptation to knock other candidates, as in knocking the old pro or the new graduates. Instead, state that you both have strengths and then talk about your own. This is particularly true if you are a new graduate being interviewed by an old pro or even the reverse.

Judgment Questions

These are questions that force you to make a choice and in so doing to reveal some aspect of your personality. Such questions are often asked to assess how big a priority your career is or whether you are flexible or dogmatic when it comes to applying company policy. Judgment questions are difficult because the correct answer is determined by the corporate culture and the type of person they are looking for. Your attempt to gain information on either of these areas in advance by talking to other employees is the best clue to performing well on judgment questions.

In constructing and practicing your responses, be certain to include your real feelings in your response. If you don't, you'll only be tripped by your inconsistency in other parts of the interview.

SAMPLE QUESTION: "What's more important, your family or your career?"

ANALYSIS: A classic among unfair questions. If you immediately blurt out: "Family!" you've just placed your potential employer in second place, not a good move during a job interview. On the other hand, if you relegate those whom you usually profess to love like life itself to second place, even for the moment, you come off as an expedient cad.

For most of us, both family and career are important at times, and herein lies the nucleus of an effective answer to this question. For women, this question can take on a sharply sexist edge as a not-too-veiled, "So will you be having a baby and leaving us?" question. While no amount of legislation can prevent such blatantly sexist questions from being asked behind closed doors, remember that your true feelings here are none of your prospective employer's business.

SAMPLE RESPONSE: *"I think that they are both important, each requiring major expenditures of thought, time, and effort. To succeed at both sometimes requires the shifting of those priorities from one to the other. Regardless of the answer you'd prefer to hear, I think that choosing either would be, at best, a half-truth and an oversimplification as well."*

Other Judgment Questions
SAMPLE QUESTIONS: "Suppose a company policy seemed unreasonable, would you be willing to bend the rules?"

"If you catch an employee in a lie, would you warn him (or her), or report the matter to senior management?"

Both of these questions are about your integrity and loyalty and are a usual part of interviews where the security of merchandise, money or information is an issue. Your answers should indicate that you would neither bend rules nor permit a fellow employee to engage in behavior damaging to the entire organization.

How to Talk about Money

Like the waiter who leaves the check face down on your table, most of us are a bit sheepish when it comes to discussing this essential part of any job and job interview. After all, money or the need to earn more of it may be the very reason why you're having the interview in the first place.

Put aside any discomfort you may feel as you discuss your salary and be direct and above all honest about your worth and your needs. Also, in this initial interview, keep your responses simple and to the point. Avoid mentioning benefits or retirement plans or stating demands at this time. If they are interested, all these details will be worked out later.

If you are asked for the least amount you'll take, state that you'd rather not think in terms of minimums and then name your target number. Such questions may be intended to see how badly you need the job or to see how you'll react to being put on the defensive.

SAMPLE QUESTION: "What salary do you deserve?"

ANALYSIS: This is a perfectly straightforward question that many respondents overcomplicate by failing to answer directly. The question asks for a number, and that's how it should be answered. The number should be realistic and fair to both sides.

SAMPLE RESPONSE: *"I believe that a salary of $45,000 is fair to both of us. I believe you'll agree that both my qualifications and my past salary history indicate that I merit that amount."*

ERRORS TO AVOID

Failure to respond directly and succinctly. If you don't respond with a number or if you give a lengthy justification of your qualifications along with your number, you'll communicate your discomfort and fail to get what you want.

Aiming too high or too low on the salary issue. Remember, your interviewer is probably an expert on the value of your services and may have a specific number in mind. Your goal should be to approximate that expectation or present a truly overpowering reason if you don't.

Also, note that undershooting your worth in an attempt to beat the competition is just as serious an error in the other direction. If your salary expectations are well below the standard or average for your field, a low bid will be looked at as an expression of doubt about your own ability or self-worth.

Speaking in ranges in response to a direct salary question. Stating a range is a way of saying that you are willing to work for the lower number, and it's exactly what you'll get.

Questions They Shouldn't Ask

You are probably aware that no one is supposed to ask you questions about your racial or ethnic background, politics, sexual preference, family life, age, or social life. In simulated sessions, I've asked such questions, and invariably the interview subject has said: "You can't ask that question; it's illegal or has nothing to do with the job."

While such questions are inappropriate, if not illegal, an interview is often held behind closed doors without witnesses, and offensive questions can and do get asked.

How you react is a matter of judgment and conscience. But you should plan your approach to such questions in advance. I would certainly advise putting the interviewer on notice any time you are asked a question that you find offensive or that you suspect may be illegal. The strength and tone of your reaction to such problem questions must be an individual judgment call. Some effective ways to express your concern about a particular question include, "Is this question a standard part of your company's interview practices?" and "Exactly what does this line of questioning have to do with the position for which I've applied?"

If the interviewer backs off when met with such responses, or apologizes, it's probably wise to assume you're dealing with an individual rather than an organizational problem. If he or she persists, you will have to consider whether this is an environment you really wish to join.

The Closing Question

SAMPLE QUESTION: "If you are a successful candidate, when can you start?"

ANALYSIS: Don't gloat once you hear this question. Note the "if" clause in the question and realize that in a search process involving a large number of applicants, it may be a standard item, no matter how the interview goes.

Your response should indicate that you would like to leave your prior position and employer in good order and that you'll need time to do so.

SAMPLE RESPONSE: *I'd like to give the Way-Rite people a bit of time to seek a replacement and to finish a few projects I was working on. Would two weeks be okay?*

ERRORS TO AVOID: *Any sort of flip answer.* The interview is wrapping up once you're asked this question, and there can be a tendency to relax to a greater extent than you should. At a time like this, an answer such as "How about after lunch?" or some sort of gratuitous shot at your prior employer could damage your credibility.

Handling Rejection

A couple of weeks after the job interview you may get a letter that begins with a phrase such as "We are sorry to inform you that . . ." and continues on to explain in the most vague generalities that you were rejected and someone else was hired.

Reading such worn phrases as "While your qualifications made our decision a difficult one, it was felt that . . ." can produce feelings ranging from anger to the deepest disappointment, which are all understandable and perfectly normal. It's important, however, that you not begin blaming yourself when you don't achieve the desired result.

An interview is in many ways a sales call, and as any veteran salesperson will tell you, most meetings end in no sale or a rejection, no matter how well the meeting seems to go. The fact is that most job interviews end in rejection notices for most people. Don't alter your interview behavior just because you receive one or two rejections.

In the job-hunting process, you may be interviewed by a firm that has no intention of hiring you. For example, a company may wish to promote an individual from within an organization for a particular position, but company policy or even law may require advertisement and an extensive search. The requirement will be fulfilled and the internal candidate appointed.

This scenario happens all the time, but you may be unaware of it and blame your own interview performance for the rejection. A more constructive approach would be to contact a personnel officer of that corporation to seek an evaluation of your interview performance. Not every one will be willing to meet with you under these circumstances, but those who do should provide valuable information.

Practice but Don't Rehearse

You should practice a mock interview at least five and perhaps as many as ten times before you face an interviewer. Use the questions covered in this chapter as a beginning and add any situation- or industry-specific question you can anticipate.

Practice your responses and even record, listen to, and critique your performance. Internalize your personal positive points and be certain to include them in your practice responses. If you don't internalize them, they'll seem staged, and you'll lack the flexibility you'll need if the interview strays in directions you didn't anticipate. Also be certain not to do all your practicing the day before or on the day of the interview. Such cramming for an interview will only heighten your anxiety and hinder the fluency of your performance.

Summary

I began this chapter by pointing out how little control you have over the job interview. Using the information in this chapter and developing your own versions of the sample responses should level the playing field if you are new to the interview game, and even tilt it slightly in your direction as you gain experience. If one interview doesn't go as well as you expected, learn from your missteps and you'll do better next time. Now, tell me about yourself.

Quick Review:
Job Interview Strategies

1. Make sure your résumé adds up chronologically and contains dates.
2. Study an annual report or any other material that gives you advance knowledge of the company, its objectives, and its issues.
3. Don't act as if you don't need the job (unless you don't want it).

4. Practice your answers, but don't ever memorize.

5. Be ready to explain gaps in your résumé nondefensively.

6. Know your major strengths and don't be modest in discussing them.

7. Be prepared to discuss a weakness or deficiency of yours with regard to the job, but be brief, nondefensive, and matter of fact in doing so.

8. Never bad-mouth a prior employer.

9. Don't avoid numbers in discussing salary.

10. Don't let mistakes in past interviews affect your performance on future interviews. Learn from them and move on.

CHAPTER TEN

Handling the Media

AT-A-GLANCE SUMMARY

This chapter covers the tactical side of the media interview—whether television, print, or radio—and provides tips to smooth out your performance and make you more comfortable and effective in various kinds of media interviews.

You'll learn everything from where to look to how to be an assertive and directive interview subject, and you'll find out how to get the best coverage while avoiding many commonly made errors.

What You Need to Know about *All* Media Interviews

In any media interview—television, radio, or print—there are some general rules that you should keep in mind to increase the chances of *your* version of the story being reported, rather than theirs.

Have an Agenda for Your Media Interview

You would never run an important staff meeting without an agenda. You wouldn't even sit through an important dinner with a client without making a carefully worded pitch for future business. Yet corporate spokespersons routinely subject themselves to media interviews assuming that their expertise will carry them through; they do little more than wing it, even though their words will ultimately be heard by thousands or even millions of readers, viewers, and potential customers.

This "seat of the pants" approach to the media interview is why so many corporate spokespersons have a favorite "How I got burned by the media" story. The solution? Decide *exactly* what message or issue you want to get across and refer to it at every opportunity.

Having an agenda, an issue you want to get across, will give you a focus and a goal and also give you a direction in which to take the interviewer. Otherwise you'll be making the mistake of relinquishing control to the interviewer. And remember to express that agenda at every opportunity. For example, you'll often be asked by reporters and talk show hosts before a media interview begins, "What would you like to talk about?" This question is a golden opportunity to get started on getting your point across. *Never* throw that opportunity away by saying, "Anything you'd like." If you do, you're headed for an informational destination chosen by the interviewer. And since media interviewers in general avoid "feel-good" stories and issues, you might find yourself blurting out some things that will depress everything, including you, your future sales, and even your stock price.

Be Directive during the Interview

An interview is a conversation sustained by the interviewer, that is, he or she keeps it going by asking you questions. Interviewers often don't know where they are going next or how much longer they should spend on a certain topic. The subject brought up by the interviewer may not always be pertinent, and you may have a good opportunity to take the conversational ball. Here's an example of how this move would transpire:

> *Host:* "Will the new packaging developed by Blexon Industries mean more convenience for your customers?"

> *Guest:* "Yes, we think the convenience will be appreciated, but we should also be looking at the very significant benefit to the environment . . ." followed by a single example of environmental impact.

This kind of aggressive approach is not only permissible within the interview, but a necessity if you are to be effective in terms of accomplishing your informational goals.

Sometimes guests leave interviews thinking they did not reach their informational goal or get to the target issues because the host did not ask them the right questions. Remember that the host has different goals than yours, and you are unlikely to get asked "just the right questions."

By being directive with your responses, using the R.E.S.T. technique (see Chapter 6), especially on key questions, and actually naming the issues that should be discussed, you exercise a greater degree of control over the structure and direction of the interview.

Always Have an Answer to the Question, "Anything You'd Like to Add?"

As the interview comes to a close, another question is, "Anything you'd like to add?" or "Any final comments?"

This question represents your chance to present a take-home point or to restate your target issue. Yet many interviewees throw away this opportunity. Once again, audiences remember most what they hear last. With this in mind, you may want to consider repeating your most important target issue.

Plan and rehearse your response to this question in advance, and yours will be a more powerful interview.

How Long Should My Answers Be?

We're not used to long speeches or long responses on television. We've been conditioned to short bursts of information. Long or multilayered responses are one of the fastest ways to get a viewer to tune out.

As a general guide, answers to questions should range from fifteen to no more than thirty seconds, with no more than ten seconds on follow-up responses. In fact, for the stand-up TV interview, I recommend shortening your response to about fifteen seconds. Don't feel hamstrung by this rule, but use it as a guideline.

Learn to systematize your response technique following the R.E.S.T. formula (described in Chapter 6). In this manner, you'll cover the material, get to your target issues, and appear concise and knowledgeable.

Certainly, there are issues of such complexity that a ten- or fifteen-second response becomes impractical. Remember, however, that your ultimate audience (the viewer) is, rightly or wrongly, accustomed to being fed a diet of short answers (also known as sound bytes).

Getting Comfortable on Television

One of the most insidious phrases in media is the one that used to open countless TV shows in the early days of the medium: "And now, through the magic of television, we bring you another episode of . . ."

Today, one of the reasons you'd prefer four hours of dental drilling to sitting through a five-minute media interview is that you still think there's something magical about television. It seems like a world in which everything is perfect or close to it. Most of the people you see on television meet the cultural norms of attractiveness and are articulate to the point that you almost never hear them flub a word or go blank or seem anxious or even seem to have suffered a bad day.

Commercials are perfect and perfectly timed. No news anchor ever reads a story and says: "I didn't understand that story either; let me try to explain it so we can both understand it." A weekly moment like that on network TV would cost millions of dollars annually in time that could be sold to sponsors.

And so, with few exceptions, the spontaneity—the imperfections and, some would argue, the humanity—has drained out of TV programming. Newscasters read teleprompters between commercials and chat with unparalleled awkwardness ("Great story, Judy!") only when the show is running short. For me, the starched world of TV journalism is summarized in a line uttered by the late actor Ted Knight, the vapid but well-meaning news anchor Ted Baxter on *The Mary Tyler Moore Show,* who said, "In this just handed me, there is something on your tooth."

The only thing that television shares with the world of magic is that they are both based on illusion. In this section, with the objective of making you comfortable on camera, the medium of television will be demystified so that you can use this important medium effectively rather than buying into the passé notion of "the magic of television."

At the Studio

If you have not visited a television studio before, you will be in for a few sensory surprises. It will be much smaller than it appears on the air. The rest of what happens while you are there has little to do with your comfort and everything to do with making you look and sound as good as you can, so don't be put off or unnerved about what you are going to experience.

To begin with, you will be asked to sit on a cramped platform in a chair on the set next to the host's chair or desk that is often higher than yours. You will be told to relax, but not to move or move the chair at any time during the interview. Then they'll pin a microphone on your clothing, sometimes running wires and bits of tape around, under, and behind you to hide the microphone cord, while someone else offers you a bit of makeup regardless of your gender.

In the midst of all this, you may or may not meet the host, who will hardly say two words to you. Suddenly, someone yells "Ten seconds," the chaos becomes silence, some lights come on that you will think are hot enough to bleach your hair, and the host, who snubbed you two minutes ago, is looking engagingly into your eyes and welcoming you to *Action News*.

Just as you begin to gain your composure, you hear the host thanking you for being on *Action News*, and in a flash it's over, leaving you driving back to the office hoping it all went well, with little or no idea of what you said or how it was received.

As they say in television, let's take that again, only in slower motion, with some explanations along the way, which should make you more comfortable.

First of all, the television cameras tend to spread out or enlarge a space as seen on the screen, and therefore your chair will be a lot closer to the host than it would be in a social setting. Be assured that this proximity is for strictly optical reasons, rather than a plot to make you uncomfortable.

Remember, if you don't look good, neither does their show. The person who places the microphone will attempt to tuck the cord out of sight and keep it from pulling on you and your garments. If the microphone or cord is making you uncomfortable, ask to have it adjusted; they will be glad to help.

Particularly for the male guests, your visit to a television studio is usually the first time someone will offer you makeup. I'd strongly suggest you take them up on that offer because once those lights go on and the temperature climbs to tropical levels, your host will look as comfortable as ever while you perspire enough to look more like a suspect than a guest. Wear the makeup!

Don't Buy into the Host's Preshow Behavior

Meeting the interviewer usually goes one of two ways. Either he or she will be almost overly friendly and try to put you at ease, or virtually ignore you to the extent that you take an instant dislike to your seemingly arrogant host. Don't buy into the behavior of the former type and don't be offended by the latter.

A friendly host can be just that and can help you get in the mood for a pleasant exchange. But you can be certain that the same interviewer is capable of looking you in the eye once the cameras are on and asking you, out of the blue, to comment on the drug problem in your company.

If you remain neutral and unaffected by preshow banter or the lack of it, you will not be lulled into a false sense of security and will be better prepared to handle an adversarial interview.

As for those interviewers who generally avoid talking about the interview before it begins, this is usually a way of keeping the material fresh and spontaneous, since the chat that takes place before the interview should be of less consequence than the interview itself.

I've conducted hundreds of on-camera interviews. I'm least comfortable when I meet the guest before the show and am lulled into an extended conversation. The result is that both of us have to sit there trying to remember which part of the interview is new and which has already taken place, instead of simply having an "on the air" conversation, which I find to be the best form of interview.

Once the Interview Begins

Look at the Person You Are Talking To

Where or what do you look at while on television? On a set with three or more cameras, it may not be easy to figure out where to look. Most of us have a vague notion that the camera with the red light (tally light) is the one that's on. The confusion is heightened when your host spends some time looking at you, some time looking at the camera (particularly at the beginning of the show), and some time looking at notes.

The rule here is simple and applies to all television interviews at which the interviewer is present: *look at the person you are talking to,* not at any camera, or the wall, or the floor—just the person you're speaking to. Even if you're talking directly to the viewing audience, look at the interviewer and say something like "Your viewers would like to know that . . ."

By looking at the person you are talking to, you enable the director to give you the best coverage. If you attempt to play to the cameras, the director will have to guess where your eyes will turn up next, and you'll look either shifty or comical.

If there is a monitor (a television used by crew members for viewing the program) on the set, avoid looking at it during the program. If you have a burning desire to see how you look on TV, do so after the taping, or have someone record your appearance. (TV news operations will often, on request, provide you with a copy.) Looking at a monitor while you are being interviewed is very much like having lunch while you focus your eyes on a person at the next table.

Begin by Greeting the Host and Thanking Him or Her for the Invitation

This is a subtle way to take charge at the opening of an interview, or at least let the host know that you are thinking and in control of your own agenda.

For years at the opening of television interviews I've conducted, I've often greeted guests with the usual and somewhat perfunctory "Welcome to the program!" As I analyze the habit and why so many hosts do it, I have come to the realization that it's not just a polite greeting, but an important "test question."

If my "Welcome to the program!" is met with a blank stare and a mild affirmative nod or nervous smile, it's a clear signal that the guest is very nervous and that I'll have to provide some help in lightening the conversational load. On the other hand, if I'm an adversarial host and my "welcome" brings the same blank expression, I know that I am definitely in charge and that nailing the guest on the issues will be an easy task.

Regardless of the host's approach, begin the first response with a remark such as "Before I begin, I want to thank you for inviting me here to talk about . . ." It's a clear signal to your host that you are in charge or at least on an equal footing.

Don't Produce the Show

You will notice a number of people on the studio floor whose purpose it is to give cues and time signals to the host, or to hold up cue cards or other messages related to the smooth running of the program or interview. Remember that you are not a member of the production staff, and none of these signals, cues, or cards applies directly to you, nor do you know what they mean.

For example, some guests will be in the middle of a response and see a card being held up that says: "10 seconds." Suddenly that guest becomes a self-appointed "producer" and hurries his or her response.

The fact is that if someone holds up a sign that says "10 seconds" or gives a hand signal that seems to suggest a speed-up in the proceedings, you don't really know what it means. Are there ten seconds remaining to the next commercial? The end of the program? Or even thirty seconds remaining but the host likes an early reminder? You don't know and you shouldn't care.

Have a conversation with your host and concentrate on getting your target issues in, as well as your theme. If you let the host and the production staff do their jobs, yours will be a more effective and credible appearance.

Handling That First Question

In a nonadversarial interview, or at least one in which the interviewer wants you to feel comfortable, you might be told what the first question will be, or, if there is more than one guest, the host may let you know who will be getting the opening question. It's been my experience that this relaxes guests and lets them do a better job, particularly in the opening of the program.

Let's take a look at the opening of the show from another perspective, one in which the host is adversarial. Assume that you are a spokesperson for a company that has had an environmental accident. You're there to explain the situation and provide reassurance for the viewers. Realize that the interviewer will be biased toward the audience and, at least for a portion of the program, even hostile to you.

One trick such a host will play is to soothe your nerves just before the show by telling you that he or she will open the program with a question about your company's history. As you may have already guessed, as soon as the theme music subsides, the opening question you are likely to get is (remember the audience bias), "How long do you and your band of polluting rip-off artists intend to go on destroying the environment?"

In the face of such a question, a strong and immediate denial is the best solution ("Bill, you've got your facts wrong. First of all . . .").

Don't Bring Notes

One unfair tradition that has evolved over the years in TV interviewing is that guests don't get to use notes. The host can be encamped at a desk covered by note cards, in a studio festooned by cue cards reminding him or her of everything from your name to that of the sponsor, but you are left to sit there "naked" without a desk or so much as a legal pad.

You may view this situation as a disadvantage, but given the level of information usually covered in a television interview and the fact that you are the expert, you really have little need for notes. If certain dates are important, do your best to remember or approximate, if that won't cause difficulty. Realize that the viewer remembers little of the content of the television interview, so keep your remarks general and nontechnical.

Once again, your emphasis should be on accomplishing your informational goals and getting your theme or agenda across, not on presenting an oration that explores the most minute details of your position(s). Relax and remember that you are the expert.

If yours is a business that will be better explained through the use of graphs or other visuals during your interview, make sure they are in a form compatible with the technical requirements of the broadcast studio. Remember that not all studios and programs are set up to handle graphics and that their successful inclusion in your interview requires some technical rehearsal and a decision as to when they will be used.

What's Your Phone Number?

Don't get tripped up by this obvious question. You may have seen an old episode of the classic Jackie Gleason sitcom, "The Honeymooners," in which Ralph Kramden, after exhaustive study of obscure operatic arias, fails immediately and dismally on a quiz show because he can't recognize the melody to "Swanee River." Poor Ralph did what many interview guests do: despite elaborate preparations, he forgot the obvious.

An obvious and common question is, "It's been a pleasure to have you with us today, and I know our viewers will want to know more. Is there a phone number they can call?"

It sounds like the simplest of questions, yet since you never call yourself, or if your company has a customer 800 number that you never use, it's altogether possible that you'll have no idea what number the viewer should call.

Worse, if you respond by saying you don't know or can't remember the number, especially since this question occurs at the end of the show, your authority and credibility as a spokesperson will suffer.

The solution? Prearrange with the producer to have your phone number superimposed on the screen during your appearance. If you aren't precisely sure of your number, suspend the "no notes" rule, and write the number on a small index card. When asked the number, just mention that you've written it down to make sure you get it right, and read it off the card. Accuracy is crucial at a moment like this, and both your host and your viewers will appreciate this attention to detail.

If You Make an Error

Over the course of a five- and especially a fifteen-minute or longer interview, you may make some kind of content error, such as getting a number wrong or substituting a word. What should you do?

First of all, what you shouldn't do is make that error the focus of your thoughts for the rest of the interview. If you do so, you will no longer be listening fully to the subsequent questions, and your performance for the rest of the interview will suffer.

The solution here is a judgment call. If the error was minor, let it go uncorrected. As I've pointed out before, audiences remember little of the content they hear in the media interview unless it's out of the ordinary, and your saying that you made an error is out of the ordinary. You have to weigh the importance of correcting the error against saying that you made a mistake and what that costs in terms of credibility. Once again, unless it is a serious error, my advice would be to let it go.

If you're uncomfortable with that advice, you can use the final seconds of the interview, if you get the "Anything you'd like to add?" question. Do not, however, in these crucial closing seconds of your appearance use words such as "I made a mistake earlier." Instead, use a remark such as "I'd like to *clarify* something I said earlier . . ." In this manner, the viewer's impression is likely to be that you are interested in making your message as clear and accurate as possible, rather than that you screwed up and are trying to cover yourself or at least that part of yourself.

The Very End

One of my goals in this book is to prevent you from making many of the embarrassing errors made by speakers of all skill and experience levels. One of these errors commonly occurs at the very end of a sit-down media interview.

As the theme music comes up and the lights dim and your host has said the last good-bye, a technician is *supposed* to cut power to your microphone so that any words you say will not be heard over the credits. More than one media personality has ended a career or become a feature of blooper albums by making a remark, sometimes off-color, while thinking the mike was dead.

For example, there is the oft-told story of "Uncle Don," who in decades past was the host of a popular children's program. At the end of the final broadcast (and it was this remark that made it the final broadcast), Uncle Don, after saying good-bye to his young fans, thinking his microphone was off, became a broadcast immortal, albeit an unemployed one, by saying, "That ought to hold the little bastards."

Your potential blunder here is not likely to be of such catastrophic proportions, but I have had guests say things over the credits such as,

"Are we done?" or "That wasn't so bad," or "How did I do?" (Fine, until you asked that question!)

The usual rule? Don't utter a word during the closing credits or when the lights dim, until a studio member says "Clear" (the usual signal that a studio is off the air).

Also watch your nonverbals at the end of the show. Sometimes, to relieve pent-up tension, guests may shake their heads, laugh, or even bury their heads in their hands in mock exhaustion. The problem is that after the viewer sees and hears a credible, effective interview, your nonverbals could undermine your entire performance. All in all, it's best to assume that the TV interview ends when you leave the studio or even the building.

The Stand-Up or On-the-Scene TV Interview

Sometimes you don't go to the media, they come to you, in the form of a stand-up or on-the-scene interview. These are often prerecorded, but with currently available technology, they are just as easily done live. Stand-up interviews, like press conferences, tend to occur under negative circumstances.

In addition, if it's a breaking story, reporters are likely to be more aggressive than usual in hopes of giving the story a "late-breaking" or exclusive quality. A few important rules and strategies will help get you through what many consider a stressful situation.

Maintain Control of the Interview

This is not as difficult as it sounds. First of all, if a bunch of reporters come at you, thrusting microphones and shouting questions and competing for recognition, don't even try to respond (but don't walk away either).

Instead, calmly tell the reporters to please move back, ask one question at a time, and slow down or you can't possibly continue the interview. Making these requests calmly will change the tone of the interview from a veritable shouting match (which you will lose) to more of a press conference, where you have a better chance of telling your story.

You also want to appear calm and in charge, in the event that your interview is being fed back to the studio for live broadcast. Realistically, no one will move back (they need the tight shots) but you will get gentler treatment if you *calmly* express your discomfort.

Know to Whom You Are Speaking

Especially if you're not the regular media spokesperson for your company, ask reporters to identify themselves as they question you. In this instance, you'll have a bit more think-time, and it's been my experience that people (even reporters) tend to be more polite after they have just told you who they are. By the way, never hesitate to ask for press credentials (usually issued by local police departments or governments). Especially when you are new at talking to the media, you have the right to make certain that you are talking to a reporter and not an investigator for a competitor or legal adversary.

If You Can't Talk Now, Say Why

Don't just walk away, or they'll put your "escape" on the air. Reporters who come on the scene to get a story are in serious pursuit of news, and they don't like meeting up with a smug, uncaring spokesperson. If that's the way you play it, that's the way you'll be covered.

If there's a good reason you can't talk now, simply say why and tell them when you will have more information. Reporters won't like this response, but if it's the truth, it won't do you any harm. If you say "no comment," it will be used on the air and do about as much for your credibility as pleading the Fifth Amendment.

Don't Treat the Interview as an Audition

Your goal should be to answer the questions asked concisely and honestly. That means you might have to think about a response or even take a second shot at having the words come out just the way you want them.

Unfortunately, many spokespersons are intimidated by the immediacy and largely self-imposed pressure of having to think on their feet. Therefore, the stand-up interview runs the risk of becoming an audition in which you try to answer every question with total fluency and dazzling brilliance, topping off each with your most engaging smile.

If you can manage to pull this off, you're making two mistakes. First and most seriously, you are no longer thinking, you are performing. Second, you are focusing on image rather than on content, and you can be virtually assured that in so doing you will make serious misstatements.

Take your time, think about your responses, and don't let the reporter or the presence of cameras or lights cause you to rush your answers. If none of that motivates you, remember that the more time you spend on each response, the fewer questions you'll have to answer, especially in a live interview.

If You Make a Mistake, Stop Talking

While you need not slip into apoplexy if you misstate your case or get halfway through a statement that you realize is incorrect, hopelessly awkward, or laced with a piece of information you suddenly realize you shouldn't have revealed, simply stop talking *immediately*, and, without saying why, ask to restate the response. The reporter will have little choice but to let you do it again, and you will end up with a better interview.

If you make the mistake of completing a response you don't want used, you'll have to depend on the reporter not to use it. Compounding the problem, the story may be assembled for broadcast by someone other than the reporter who did the interview, and the wrong response may be aired against your wishes.

Therefore, waiting until the conclusion of the interview to ask for a retake of one of the responses will bring only a polite refusal, or, as they pack up and move on to the next story, a chillingly insincere reassurance that "It was fine." This response will, of course, leave you frozen in terror until the story airs.

Once again, if you make a serious error in a stand-up interview, protect your interests by stopping your response immediately and asking for a retake. The same rule applies even if you find yourself uncomfortable or just too tense to continue the response. Stop and begin again. You'll be more relaxed and better able to give a correct and effective response.

Conclude and Exit Gracefully

I am frequently asked how you know when the stand-up interview is over or how to end the encounter. If there is only one reporter present, the interview will probably end with a thank you and a request for a number at which you can be reached for further information.

Once the questions become repetitive, it is a good time to end the proceedings. However, do not simply walk away, leaving any of the reporters in mid-question. If you do, you run the risk of having a snubbed reporter go back to the studio, play the recording of your exit, and claim that you refused to answer his or her question.

Avoid this trap by saying that you'll have to end the interview at this time, but that you will be available in the event of further developments. If you have no more time to submit to questions, by all means say so, but exit gracefully and on a courteous note.

A Final Word on Stand-Up Interviews

If you are a regular media spokesperson, you will become quite facile at handling the stand-up interview. If you are not the usual designee for such interviews, you will find your first stand-up interview rather unnerving. (Many first-timers report that they had no idea what they said until they saw themselves on the evening news.)

Avoid or lessen your level of anxiety by practicing these interviews in advance. An afternoon spent with your colleagues conducting and recording mock stand-up interviews will pay handsome dividends when it comes time to face the cameras for real.

The Remote-Camera Interview

The remote-camera interview is an interview in which the reporter or interviewer is not there in front of you; he or she may be in the next room or even in another city. It's a staple of all of the cable news networks when they have an on-air guest from another city or even another country.

Typically, you will be seated in front of a camera, hooked up to a microphone, and given an earpiece through which you will hear the audio portion of the program (including questions for you as well as statements of the other guests). Whether you are able to see the program depends on whether there is a monitor present.

You're Always "On the Air"

The key to an effective performance in the remote-camera interview is twofold. First, once you sit in the chair, assume you are "live" and on the air. You might be told that you'll be on in five minutes and literally find a question coming at you five seconds later. That's why more than one subject of this type of interview has popped onto the screen in the middle of a contact lens or toupee adjustment and spent the rest of the program wishing he or she were on one of Saturn's rings instead of in that chair.

Listen Closely, Very Closely

A second key to an effective remote camera interview is listening to the *entire* program, including segments in which you are not supposed to appear. This becomes difficult, because after you are introduced you might find yourself off the air for quite an interval as other guests talk and even as commercial breaks of several minutes' duration go by. Unless you actively listen and become involved in the conversation when it's your turn to participate, your responses won't be as sharp as they should be, as you struggle to get up to speed.

As you participate in the interview or discussion, look directly into the camera, both while you are questioned and as you respond. As you may have observed, some guests have a tendency to feel that they are alone or to act as if they are talking on the telephone during this type of interview, and will perhaps look to the heavens during a question as if checking with the deity on how to respond. Once again, look at the camera as you are questioned and as you respond.

Don't Be Too Polite

If the program on which you are doing the remote camera interview is a debate or you are teamed with a guest who opposes your interests, remember that this gathering has been arranged by the producers in the hope that some verbal sparks will fly.

If the situation is adversarial, in addition to telling your side of the issue, a further objective should be to get the most air time. One obvious way is to disagree immediately with your adversary by interrupting him or her at any time an error of fact is made, even if you are not on camera. Interrupting will usually get you on camera and, if you don't carry things so far as to elicit an admonition from the host, you'll end up with most of the air time to promote *your* point of view.

Producers and interviewers often appreciate this kind of spirited debate, but the specifics of how much is tolerable are a function of the usual policy on that program. If you do interrupt another guest, do so deliberately but unemotionally, because, just as in any other debate, if you lose your temper, you've lost the debate, even if the facts tend to be on your side.

A more subtle way to get air time and steal your opponent's thunder is to react nonverbally to your adversary. Nodding, frowning, or smiling incredulously during a point being made by your opponent is a much more interesting shot for a director who must choose from among some "talking heads."

Call-In Radio Programs

Just about when audiences had given up on AM radio in favor of the higher fidelity sounds of the FM band, AM made a super-strong come-back with the resurgence of talk radio, particularly in the form of the call-in radio show.

The overwhelming popularity of this format has created an equally overwhelming demand for guests, which in turn increases the likelihood of your making one of these appearances as a media spokesperson. The following simple tips will increase your chances for a successful performance.

The first immediate difference between radio and television is that radio is much more informal. Time and timing are often less crucial, especially in a non-network or local appearance, and the conversations, questions, and responses are likely to be a lot less structured and more free flowing. What you have so far is a recipe for pulverizing boredom unless a few ingredients are added. These usually include a host who will make more than occasional stabs at being controversial and callers intent on putting the guest (or even the host) on the griddle.

In talk radio, the game is as much one of entertainment as it is infor-mation, and if you are the guest, you might find yourself the victim of that entertainment as the host sides with an irate caller against you.

Don't be put off by the way the host promotes your appearance on the program as you hear statements such as, "And after the news, some-one from Metro Transit Railway will be here to tell us why lateness is their most important product!"

Sure, you should disagree with such foolery on the part of your host, but his or her objective is to keep people from dialing around, and it's been proved that controversy, even if simulated, is a much better audience-grabber than a verbal love feast.

While it may be the host's job to stir up controversy, as in any media interview it's your job to get your message across. In the talk-radio arena this means not just rolling with the punches, which are certain to be there, but having a theme to which you can keep coming back, so that while the audience is entertained, it is also exposed to your message and your theme.

As in other mass-media forms, repetition builds retention. (This is how you learned the lyrics to that song you hate but they keep playing on the radio.) The same type of imprinting goes on with your audience if you have a theme and come back to it whenever possible. ("Amalgamated Power Company has low electric rates!")

Bring Your Notes

You are likely to be asked a wide array of questions on a call-in program and, especially in local markets where the demand for program material is high and guests are not that plentiful, program segments are likely to run anywhere from one half hour to one hour.

Make sure your notes are on index cards (large cards are easier to read) and arranged according to subject. Using cards is important, because listeners will find it hard to believe that they are talking to an expert if they hear paper rattling each time you are asked a question.

What should your notes contain? Any type of detailed information that you have difficulty remembering, such as dates, prices, phone numbers, hot-line numbers, and the like. Also be sure not to put too much information on a card. Stick to short phrases and key words so you'll converse rather than read.

Treat Callers with Respect, Even if
They Don't Do the Same for You

The people who call radio programs have widely varying informational needs. As any host will tell you, those same callers also seem to have just as widely varying degrees of intelligence, sanity, and even sobriety.

No matter what kind of caller you get, you are better off trying to give a serious response than tossing out a line such as, "Have another beer and call later, Bill." In an awkward moment with a difficult caller, your main concern should be the rest of your audience, not just that caller. You want to leave the impression that you are a serious spokesperson with a worthwhile message.

If things get out of hand, count on the host to deal with obnoxious questioners. He or she might let an irate caller batter you a bit for the sake of entertainment, but ultimately the host wants the show to be taken seriously and will come to your rescue. Remain respectful and informative and let your host handle the verbal fisticuffs that sometimes typify talk radio.

The Press Interview

An interview by a newspaper reporter from the print media may be held in your office and have a predetermined running time and agenda. These are factors that should serve to make you more comfortable, but they are also factors that could serve to trip you up if you're not careful.

Plan Ahead

The comfortable surroundings can have you off your guard and make you a lot more casual (and talkative) than you would be on a TV news set. As in other interviews, have a theme and target issues to which you can keep coming back. Not having a preset theme for the interview will result in your bringing up many more issues than you intended. More important, lack of planning and focus in the issues area will give the reporter's perception a much larger role in deciding which aspects of the story should be emphasized.

Record Your Interview

Many print reporters, with your permission, will routinely turn on a recorder at the beginning of their interview and state that they do so for the sake of accuracy and as backup for their notes. Should this bother you? Not at all. In fact, if the reporter can go back and check the recording as he or she writes the story, quotes are all the more likely to be accurate.

I'd further recommend, whether or not the reporter records the interview, that you make your own recording, with the explanation that it's your policy to record all such interviews. Not only does your own copy of the interview provide a valuable reference source, should you need it, but the reporter who goes back to the office to write the story is likely to be extra careful in assembling that story, knowing that you have a recorded copy of the session.

Control the Agenda

You lose control of the interview when you forget that *you* and not the reporter are the expert and you fail to establish a viewpoint as to what is and is not important to the story being covered.

Remember, in an interview with a TV or radio reporter, the material that goes on the air consists mainly of your voice and words, so you have some control over the emphasis and direction of the story.

In a press interview, the conversational format can obscure the points that you want emphasized. In fact, if the reporter's perception of what is important differs from yours, and you fail to correct it, you're inviting a story that will bear little resemblance to what you said in the interview.

Executives I've spoken to who have had a negative experience with a print reporter often admit, if grudgingly, that they failed to control the agenda by specifically labeling some facts as more important than others. Instead, they just sat there answering questions, a sure way to let the reporter decide what's important and what's not.

Remember, even if the reporter has a preconceived slant on the story, you, as the expert, have the power to change it by emphasizing *your* side of things.

To summarize the planning process for the print interview, make sure you have an agenda and a target issue or issues you want to get across to the reporter. Attempt to work those target issues into your responses.

Once the interview is under way, be certain to advocate your position by emphasizing the responses you consider central to the issue under discussion.

Also, don't hesitate, particularly with underinformed reporters, to tell them if their approach or perspective in covering a story is simply wrong. Finally, give the interview emphasis through repetition of important responses and clarify technical or complex issues.

It Ain't Over, Even When It's Over

Unlike a baseball game, a print interview is always an extra-inning affair—that is, the reporter doesn't stop thinking when the notebook closes. The interview subject usually does, however. The reporter may still be looking for an angle or a way to get into the story, such as an interesting quote or headline.

In contrast, you are so relieved that the interview is over and has concluded successfully that your guard is down, and that degree of self-inhibition that served you so well during the interview—what I call your "edit circuit"—is shut down. It's at a moment such as this that you can blurt out that headline.

For example, an electric-company spokesman told a reporter of a power failure caused by a squirrel that had gotten into a transformer. While leaving the interview, the reporter ventured the line, "You really fried that sucker." The spokesperson's nodding agreement of that remark made it the headline of the story: "WE REALLY FRIED THAT SUCKER"—hardly a comment to endear the company to animal lovers.

The point here is to be careful. It's the reporter's job not just to get the story, but to present it with an angle that will grab the reader's attention. Sometimes adding a bit of flash to a headline may be at your expense.

Remember, the print interview is over when the reporter has left your presence, not merely when he or she has closed the notebook or shut off the recorder. The reporter is always thinking, so be certain to do the same; remember your agenda and target issues, and especially remember not to kid around at the end, lest your frivolity end up as the headline.

What To Do about Reporter Errors

Despite your best efforts and even those of the TV and print reporters who cover your story, mistakes such as factual errors, wrong names, and misquotes sometimes get into print and on the air. Just before writing these words, I viewed some television coverage of the crash of a military jet in which the reporter described the severity of the fire as being the result of "all that high-octane fuel." (Jet aircraft burn kerosene.)

If you are wronged in print or on the air, assess how serious the error is. A mispronounced name or a wrong title may not be trivial to you, but most viewers or readers are not that concerned about your story. In such cases, call the reporter and ask him or her to correct the item in the file for future reference.

If it's a more serious error, such as a statement that, if left uncorrected, could cause damage to your product, company, or company image, call the reporter and request that a correction be aired or printed. Be polite but firm. That is, point out the seriousness of the situation and request that it be corrected, but don't expect more than a correction of the error, especially since it was undoubtedly just that, an innocent error.

If these steps fail, contact the editor (print) or producer or news director at a TV or radio station and repeat your request. Complaining about reporters has about the same effect as complaining to a department chairman about an ineffective college professor. The fact is that one complaint doesn't usually get results. But if a reporter's name keeps popping up in sentences that also contain the word "inaccuracy," you can be assured that some action will be taken.

Summary

The people who occupy the anchor desks, particularly those with seven-figure salaries, would probably like you to believe that participating in a media interview is a difficult or at least highly specialized activity—right up there with vascular surgery or night-carrier landings. There is nothing all that difficult about the media interview. Sure, for most of us it's a different environment, but nothing that should inspire any degree of awe or reverence.

If you remember that *you* are the expert, and they are not, and practice a few media interviews, treating them more as conversations than as inquisitions, you should be well equipped to handle things once the "on-the-air" light flashes.

Quick Review:
Successful Media Interviews

1. Don't buy into the host's pre-interview behavior.

2. Look at the person you're talking to, not the camera (except in the remote camera interview).

3. Once on the air, ignore time signals. They are for your host, not for you.

4. Begin any in-studio interview with a "Thanks for inviting me" statement.

5. Use notes on radio, but not on television.

6. Keep your answers brief.

7. Try to direct your interview to your agenda or target issues.

8. In stand-up interviews, know to whom you're talking.

9. Don't let reporters rush you.

10. Make your own recording of all print interviews.

CHAPTER ELEVEN

Preparing to Be an Effective Witness

AT-A-GLANCE SUMMARY

This chapter is intended to give you the information you need to be an effective communicator on the witness stand, whether in a legal proceeding or a regulatory or legislative hearing. You'll discover how to avoid the various traps and tricks the opposition may set for you and still maintain your credibility.

Most important, this chapter encourages you to listen to your counsel and leave the strategizing about the case to him or her while you answer only the questions you are asked.

In Chapter 10 I pointed out the increasing likelihood that in your capacity as a corporate manager or executive, you will be interviewed by the media. This is a type of exposure some of us not only welcome but actually relish.

Unfortunately, another communicative forum that you are also increasingly likely to encounter is the witness stand. If you work in a regulated industry, you'll probably wind up testifying before a legislative or regulatory committee or commission.

The witness stand requires a special set of communicative skills for you to survive and prosper in an adversarial system in which the wrong word or phrase, the impression you leave, or even what you don't say, can have dire consequences.

This chapter does not give you legal advice (you should get that from your lawyer), but rather acquaints you with some of the strategies that can be employed against you on the witness stand and how to combat them successfully. With the advice of your counsel, plenty of practice, and application of the information provided in this chapter, you should be able to improve your chances greatly for a credible, effective appearance on the witness stand.

Getting the Most from Your Legal Counsel

Let Your Attorney Handle the Case Strategy

Remember, witnesses don't win cases, attorneys do. Everyone loves winning. It's a natural tendency when you're involved in a legal case to try to do what you can to contribute to a victory. As a witness, however, it's not your role to strategize. Rather, it's your role to answer the questions you are asked, truthfully and to the best of your ability. It's your attorney's job to object and attempt to prevent certain lines of questioning, or to present witnesses who can refute testimony that may be damaging to your case.

If you attempt to help the case by giving an evasive or partial answer or saying you don't know, when it can be easily proved that you do, you may actually be interfering with your counsel's planned strategy. In addition, you are tampering with your most valuable asset on the stand, *your credibility.*

Particularly if you are a witness in a large, complicated case such as a regulatory hearing, which may last for weeks, you are likely to be present for only a small part of the proceeding and hear only a limited portion of the testimony. This puts you in a poor position to grasp the overall strategy in the case and hardly in a position to score points for your side.

Trying to win a case as a witness by being uncooperative with the opposing counsel can also backfire another way: perhaps your area of testimony is one in which your counsel expects to incur some damage that he or she intends to counter later in the proceeding. Telling a witness this would be like telling a boxer that he is likely to get knocked out in the next round but to get in there and fight.

Trust Your Legal Counsel

Attorneys might actually help you by not telling you the whole story. For example, if your testimony is a problem part of the case, you might never know it. You will be most helpful in such situations if you merely answer the questions asked and call less attention to this part of the case than you would by being contentious with your questioner.

A legal proceeding can be compared to a checker game, with the witnesses being the checkers and the attorneys the players who move the checkers around the board. You really can't see the other checkers, nor do you have a firm idea of your position on the board. If checkers on a board could make their own moves, the result would be chaos. When witnesses start acting on their own, the result is much the same, maybe not chaos, but certainly not victory.

Trusting your counsel to provide the game plan and answering the questions you are asked is your job as a witness, not trying the case yourself.

Tell the Truth

Aside from ethical considerations and the fact that you are generally under oath as a witness and thus subject to a possible perjury charge, there is another reason to tell the truth that should impress even the most ruthless and expedient witness: lying doesn't work. Have you ever noticed that while most people will tell you that they are basically honest, they will also admit to telling the occasional "white lie"? We've all heard them, from "My dog ate my homework," to the more elaborate, but equally ridiculous, "We'd love to have dinner with you on Friday, but we are having a small memorial service to commemorate the death of our goldfish." While these little lies may be a part of life, they never really fool us, even as we nod in mock sympathy at tellers of such fibs.

Most of us are good at spotting deception, whether the signal is an averted glance or a slight quaver in the voice, but for the sake of being polite, we let it go. Juries, judges, and regulatory bodies, however, make their decisions outside the bounds of the social politeness that permits us to accept a certain degree of deception. Honesty is definitely the best policy, especially on the witness stand.

Now that I've convinced you to listen to your attorney and impressed you with the need to tell the truth, here are some techniques you can use in depositions and trial hearings to enhance your effectiveness as a witness.

Depositions

Most of our images of witnesses and witness behavior have been shaped by television courtroom dramas, from *Perry Mason* to *Law & Order*. Some interesting and fact-based situations are portrayed, but one thing the media attorneys never seem to do is conduct a deposition.

A deposition is an information-gathering interview conducted by the opposition in the presence of your attorney prior to a court proceeding. It's not the giveaway it seems, because as the other side is asking you questions, they may be giving clues to your attorney as to the areas in which they lack information as well as their overall strategy in pursuing a case.

Your attorney will be present at a deposition to object to the questions that he or she feels you should not have to answer. At the same time, you should remember that you are there to provide information and to answer questions under your counsel's guidance.

The deposition is a research expedition in which the sides in a case find out about each other. The best course in answering is to seek the advice of your attorney, not by waiting for a nod of approval before each of your responses, but by pausing for a possible objection, which will give you information on the problem with the question being asked.

Your attorney will generally allow greater latitude in a deposition than in a trial or regulatory proceeding because he or she is also gaining information on areas the opposition intends to explore. As you respond, an experienced attorney can spot strategies being developed by the opposition, so don't feel you are giving away the store by answering their questions.

As in any legal proceeding, you should tell the truth (you will be under oath) while keeping your answers brief and to the point.

Remember that if you yourself object to a question or inquire as to its relevance instead of responding, you are also informing the other side that this particular area is a sensitive one that you'd rather not talk about. Also remember that this kind of defensive behavior on your part, or any argumentative behavior for that matter, is a sure way to invite more questions on and greater interest in that very area.

Remain matter of fact, listen to your attorney's objections, and respond truthfully, briefly, and unemotionally. In this manner, you'll provide the information to which the opposition is entitled, while serving or at least not damaging your own interests.

Depositions often begin with a standard series of "identification" questions that include your name and address or prior addresses. Further questions might range into such areas as your educational background and credentials (particularly if you are testifying as a corporate official or in some other professional capacity), your marital status, and details about prior legal proceedings in which you have participated.

In some depositions, the questions may seem not only irrelevant but even trivial. In such cases, your best strategy is to avoid becoming irritated or argumentative and to continue responding. One possibility here is that the opposition is gathering a body of information in which they hope to find the tiniest inconsistencies or inaccuracies. These discrepancies will then be used to question your credibility during later proceedings or your ability to provide accurate testimony. This strategy can be employed when the evidence is not on the opposition's side.

Three Ways to Safeguard Your Credibility

There are three ways to combat such attempts to reduce your credibility.

The first and obvious one is to aim for total accuracy (which is easier if you keep your answers brief).

Second, take your time in responding and refer directly to documents rather than relying on memory. (Be sure and check with your attorney as to which documents to bring to a deposition, or any proceeding, as they can sometimes become evidence.)

Third, especially for detailed areas of testimony in which you are relying on memory, you should make frequent use of such phrases as "as best I can remember" or "to the best of my recollection."

Such phrases are particularly important when the opposition deliberately tries to fragment your response by asking, "So that's your entire answer?"

"As best as I can remember" gives you some latitude in a subsequent proceeding, should you need it. A simple yes-or-no response will give the opposition an opportunity to imply that you deliberately omitted information in your deposition, thus diminishing your credibility.

Truthfully including such phrases as "to the best of my recollection" or "if my memory serves me correctly" will give your attorney room to maneuver and counterattack, should your credibility be questioned based on your deposition responses, especially in terms of inadvertent inconsistencies caused by lapses in memory.

Once again, in deposition testimony, your attorney will lay out the basic structure and probably the content for you. Look at this session as you would any other interview. Answer truthfully, concisely, and unemotionally, and your counsel will probably gain as much information about the strategy of the opposition as the opposition gains for its case file.

Testifying at Trials and Hearings

Be an Active Listener

As a witness, you should listen carefully and actively to the questioner. This means looking at and even turning in the direction of that questioner and being fully tuned in to what that questioner is saying. Allowing yourself to be distracted or noticing that someone at the opposition's table is writing furiously each time you speak (which could be a planned distraction, or just the lunch order) means that you will lose your focus on the question being asked.

If you don't listen fully to the question, you are more likely to answer it incorrectly and give the opposing counsel the chance to say, "You still haven't answered my question," followed by a more strident version of that question.

By not actively listening, you permit the opposing counsel to make you appear uncooperative, and you'll end up answering two questions: the one you misunderstood and the one that was actually asked.

Seek Clarification

While you should answer the question you are asked, you shouldn't ever answer a question you don't *fully* understand. If there is a term you don't fully comprehend, or you are just confused by the question, say so.

Don't respond by saying "If I understand your question . . ." You'll be doing the work of the opposing counsel, which you shouldn't. It's possible that the questioner doesn't fully understand the issue and is merely on a fishing expedition. Instead, respond by politely saying, "I don't understand your question" and look silently and directly at the questioner. You have now put the pressure on the questioner either to clarify the question or, if he or she is unable to explain the issue, to move on to another area.

In some nonadversarial situations (for example, you're the expert talking to a regulatory board member or legislator), you might want to provide your own clarification and respond, for example, "If your question refers to vehicle emissions, what we have done in arriving at that number is . . ." In such cases it might be the wise course to educate your questioner in a constructive, nonthreatening manner.

In adversarial situations, however, let the opposition construct their own questions and don't respond until you fully understand the question. Otherwise, as mentioned above, you'll end up answering two questions: the one they asked and the one you thought they asked.

Refute Negative Language

Don't allow yourself or a situation you may be describing to be labeled in a negative way by the questioner. For example, if the question is phrased as follows: "When did you first become aware of the *complete mess* your accountants had made of the books?" and your response is "The problems with our books were noticed on . . . ," you have tacitly admitted that you have no disagreement with the "complete mess" description.

Instead, your response should refute the negative language, without repeating it, as follows: "First of all, I'll have to disagree with *your* description of our books as I point out that I reported the problems on May 19." Your attorney may object before you respond, but putting the opposition on notice that you won't passively accept their attempts at negative characterizations and descriptions will certainly cut down on their attempts to play this game.

Leave Your Temper at Home

As a questioner, if I can get you angry about questions that have no central purpose to the case or if I can get you to dislike me, when it comes time for your substantive testimony, you are more likely to react emotionally than logically. As your adversary, this is just where I want you.

This is why, when you are asked simple establishing questions about your credentials, instead of "When did you receive your bachelor's degree and what was your major?" you might hear a more antagonistic version of the same question, such as, "Exactly what is it in your background that specifically qualifies *you* for the job you have?"

If the opposition continues to ask you simple questions antagonistically, you'll be more likely to dislike the questioner and become anxious as to just how rough things will get. If sufficiently antagonized, you might find yourself locked in a game of trying to beat the questioner who's attacking your credibility. Furthermore, to the jury, judge, or other decision makers, you are likely to appear needlessly defensive or hostile.

If you are upset, you are no longer listening and no longer in control of the situation. In your angered state, you may open up new areas and show emotions that give rise to doubts about both your capability and your credibility—all this a consequence of becoming needlessly irritated by the questioner.

The best way to keep your cool on the stand is to remain psychologically neutral and not buy into the behavior of the questioner, be it hostile or overly friendly. (The overly friendly types suddenly turn on you at some point during the proceedings and achieve much the same result as the openly hostile questioner.) The questioner may play such tricks as turning his or her back on you as you respond, or conspicuously glancing at a watch as you make your point. Once the opposition realizes that you're keeping an emotional distance from behaviors designed to distract, they are more likely to stick to the case itself and allow you to do your best job as a witness.

Don't Anticipate Questions; Answer Them

When watching a film or a play, many of us like to try to figure out what happened before it actually does. Readers of "whodunit" mysteries take a particular delight in these sorts of mind games. Playing this game on the witness stand, however, is a mistake, with results that can be somewhere between unfortunate and disastrous.

On the stand, you may find yourself listening to and at the same time analyzing the questions. You may begin thinking: "I wonder where he or she is going with this line of questioning?" or "I hear this question but I know what it really means!"

The problem with either of these lines of thought is that while you are thinking, you are not fully listening to the questioner. Remember that the opposing counsel not only has the right to employ a particular strategy, but is also going to reach that all-important pivotal question whether you worry about it, anticipate it, or even try to dance away from that subject area verbally.

It's best to shut off your anticipatory circuitry and try to take the questions as they come, not as you think they'll come. To do otherwise is to listen poorly and to engage in winning the case yourself, which, as I pointed out earlier, is your counsel's job, not yours.

Don't Look Back

Just as you shouldn't listen ahead to a question and try to figure out where the questioner is going, neither should you focus on a past response that might have been in error or in which you somehow misspoke. If you do, you are no longer fully concentrating on the current question and your further responses are likely to be either wrong or misspoken.

Being a witness has some similarities to being a relief pitcher. First of all, both witnesses and relief pitchers are used only to solve a problem. In baseball the relief pitcher comes in when the starting pitcher's performance has unraveled, or if a particularly nasty hitter needs to be retired. As a witness you are brought in because a legal or regulatory problem is in need of settlement. You're both operating in a pressure-cooker situation in which mistakes will be costly.

Both the witness and the relief pitcher need to act with precision and control. As a witness, one trait you should borrow from the relief pitcher is the ability to treat questions individually, just as a relief pitcher treats batters. The really great relievers can come into a game in the late innings with runners on and no outs, give up a walk, and without looking back, go on to neutralize the next three batters. This is not accomplished by the ones who give up a walk and start agonizing about an imaginary twinge in their arm or what they might have done with that first batter. Relievers who solve the problem do so because they don't dwell on what has already transpired.

As a witness, don't look back and don't dwell on past errors or misstatements. Instead, stay in the present and focus on the question at hand. Worrying about a past response will only diminish the effectiveness of your further efforts. Rely on your counsel to minimize any damage caused by an errant response. Depending on the structure of the proceeding, your counsel may get to revisit the subject area of that problem response and make up for any lost ground.

Be Careful of Humor

In Arthur Miller's play *Death of a Salesman*, the main character, Willie Loman, is trying to explain his declining fortunes to his son: "Everybody loves a kidder, but nobody lends him any money." In other words, a sense of humor and credibility or trustworthiness are difficult if not impossible traits to convey simultaneously.

This is especially true on the witness stand, where so much of the outcome depends on which side the judge, jury, or commission members trust and believe. If such decision makers are close to deciding in your favor and you choose to deliver a humorous response to a serious question, you run the risk of losing or greatly diminishing your credibility.

On the other hand, funny issues and situations do arise in the most serious of legal proceedings. What should you do? Sit there on the witness stand doing your best Mount Rushmore imitation? Certainly not. If something funny happens you are likely to react, just as anyone would, with a smile or a degree of laughter appropriate to the situation.

The difference in your behavior as a witness, as opposed to most other communicative forums, is that *you should not initiate humor*, as in making light of a serious question or delivering a Neil Simonesque quip instead of a response. Instead, react appropriately but minimally and do your best to take every question seriously. If you do, you may not get any laughs, but the proceeding will have a much happier ending than *Death of a Salesman* does.

Be Careful of Fatigue

Despite the images fostered by the typical TV courtroom drama, the witness stand is not always the hotseat of nonstop rapid-fire verbal exchanges. Rather, it can be and often is the place from which you deliver lengthy explanations of support data or respond to numerous questions in the most minute detail. This can be particularly true in regulatory hearings where complex legal, financial, or engineering information must be explored in depth in order to begin the consideration of an outcome.

Particularly if your testimony is central to a case, you may find yourself on the witness stand for hours at a time, being asked to comment on highly specific and consequential matters. As fatigue sets in, you should be aware of its onset and ask for a recess.

Common signs of fatigue on the witness stand include:

1. Difficulty in focusing on the question or the questioner
2. Difficulty in recalling specific informational points, even those on which you are an expert
3. Losing your train of thought during a response, to the extent that you forget the question (if this happens, say so immediately)
4. Reacting emotionally rather than logically to questions

Your counsel will be on the lookout for signs of fatigue, but you should be the primary determiner of your own ability to function. If you need a break, say so immediately. You will find that even a fifteen-minute break in the action will enable you to return to the stand refreshed and ready to continue. If your counsel or the judge calls for a recess, you may have waited too long—they may have acted because you made an obvious gaffe on the stand. Recognizing and dealing with the signs of fatigue is just as important for a witness as giving truthful testimony.

Damage done to a case because a witness wasn't paying attention, or answered partially because of fatigue, is difficult to undo. When fatigue sets in, put aside that "the show must go on" mentality and have your counsel request a recess or request one yourself.

Give Your Attorney a Chance to Object

On the stand, there is the tendency for honest witnesses to want to do well. If you are testifying as a part of a corporate effort, many of your peers or senior associates may be present. Under such pressures, you may respond rather quickly, as if to show everyone present just how sharp you really are.

This is a bad time to try to impress your colleagues, and also, by not pausing before each response, you are causing a serious problem for your counsel that might even damage your case. That is, your counsel might object to a particular question and wish to have the question withdrawn. Note that the objection is to the question itself, not to your response.

If your attorney's objection is made over your response, even the most astute observer will think that your counsel was trying to shut you up. Thus, the result of the objection in the minds of the decision makers is not that there was something wrong with the question, but that you had something to hide and your attorney was concerned enough to object *over* your response. Remember, pause before you respond.

Listen to Your Counsel's Objections

An objection in court gets everyone's immediate attention as all eyes fix on the presiding official to await his or her reaction. For the spectator, it's largely a question of which side will win this mini-skirmish. As a witness, it's all too easy to get caught up in the drama of the moment and become one of those spectators.

You should focus on the content of the objection itself, because it may give you important information or suggestions that can be more consequential than whether the objection is overruled or sustained. For example, an objection may contain a reminder for you to include the phrase "to the best of my memory" in your responses, or a subtle hint to restrict your responses to a specific area.

If you focus on the content of the objection rather than on the result, as most listeners will, you gain information that you can use. By focusing on the outcome, you merely gain information about the structure or direction of the proceedings, which is really noninformation for you, since, as a witness, you have no control over where the proceedings are going.

Preparing for Testimony

Your counsel will give you specific advice based on the type of case or proceeding in which you testify and which issues your legal team expects to be covered.

When a lot of written or technical evidence is involved, it will be important to review this material, making certain to familiarize yourself with its contents. You can also help your counsel in locating areas of weakness or inconsistency that are likely to come up.

As mentioned above, be certain to check with your counsel on just which written material you should take to the court or hearing room or any meeting with the opposition. In certain types of proceedings the opposition may be entitled to copies of or access to written material in your possession pertaining to the case under consideration.

Don't Memorize Testimony

Once your legal team has assembled a set of questions that they antic-ipate being asked by the other side, they may either provide you with a list of such questions or take you through a mock round of question-ing to make sure you know the material.

Rehearsing your testimony can be an effective way of increasing your comfort level, but do so with a goal of internalizing the idea that goes behind each response rather than seeking to formulate a "canned" response. Don't memorize testimony. If you do and have a memory lapse on the stand, you won't just forget the next word or line, you'll forget the entire response.

Memorized testimony will appear wooden, flat, and rehearsed to those evaluating it. Finally, if for any reason you are asked to repeat your testimony and those present are treated to a verbatim replay of your prior effort, your testimony is more likely to be perceived as a carefully produced performance than the series of honest responses it should be.

Remember, You Are the Expert

Courtrooms and hearing rooms can be intimidating places, especially for the witness. The witness boxes, elevated squeaky chairs, and other awkward surroundings in which witnesses are placed throughout our court system seem to be designed to answer the question, "Is there any way we can make this person more uncomfortable?"

Added to the hideous ergonomics, the adversarial nature of the pro-ceedings can make the whole scene all the more intimidating. The result is that you can easily forget you are a master of your own infor-mation, and you may begin to doubt what you knew as fact just before taking the stand.

Take Your Time

One way to offset the intimidating nature of the witness stand is to take your time. Of course, based on the advice given above, you are going to pause, giving your counsel the opportunity to object. Beyond that, you should be deliberate and never hasty in responding.

In testimony, just as in conversations, the speakers control each other's delivery. For example, if as a questioner I come on loud, strong, and aggressive, you are more likely to respond quickly and with a louder and more rapid delivery than you might normally employ.

Once you are aware of this game, if you maintain a natural, conversational, and deliberate style of responding, the questioner who continues with his or her loud aggressive ways looks like little more than a bully unless he or she quiets down.

So don't be bullied or rushed; instead, pause and respond in a natural conversational tone. You'll have more control over your responses and over the person who's asking the questions.

Be Wary in Referring to Documents

If you are asked to refer to a document in responding to a question, you should also take your time in locating the *exact* portion of the material to which the question refers. Take as long as you need. If either side feels a recess is appropriate, they will request one. I point this out not as a delaying tactic, but rather because witnesses, in an attempt to be considerate of everyone's time, tend to let themselves be rushed at a moment like this.

The consequences of such haste can be devastating. For example, you may be referring to the wrong information or responding to a question that is constructed on a false premise. In your haste you may misread the material and give a damaging answer based on your misunderstanding of the document. The rule here is to serve your own interests and take your time both in finding the relevant portion of a document and in reading it. You may even wish to ask for a repetition of the question once you've found the relevant material.

When You Finish Your Response, Stop Talking

Police interrogators, corporate personnel interviewers, reporters, and attorneys all know a basic fact about the people they question, which they use to great advantage: Interview subjects fear silence; to avoid it, they will talk, even without thinking.

This is why an attorney who questions you may, at the end of your perfectly adequate response, just stare silently at you as if to say, "That can't be all you have to say; you've got to be kidding!"

In fact, when most of the people who answer untruthfully are faced with such a silence they will wrongly assume the questioner knows something more and will blurt out the truth.

It's a neat trick to get more information from you, the witness; if not to uncover a concealed truth, then at least to get you to reveal new areas of information. Now that you know about it, don't get caught.

In much of life talking is success and silence is failure. On the witness stand, having the sense to sustain a silence after your response is success, and talking too much is failure.

Summary

As I said at the outset, this chapter is not intended to give you legal advice, but to look at depositions, hearings, and trials from a communicative perspective. The best-prepared case can be lost if the evidence is poorly communicated.

Review this chapter any time you are going to participate in a legal proceeding as a witness, but at all times, listen to the direction of your legal counsel.

Among the most important pieces of advice in this chapter is that as a witness, you are there to answer questions, not to engage in verbal duels with the opposition. Strategy and tactics are best left to the legal experts; when you are an effective, honest corporate witness, then you let your legal team get their job done with minimum difficulty and maximum results.

Quick Review:
Preparing to Be an Effective Witness

1. Let your counsel try to win the case. Your role as a witness is to answer the questions.

2. Tell the truth. Lying is dishonest and illegal, and it doesn't work.

3. If you don't understand the question, say so. Don't attempt to respond.

4. Leave your temper at home. Lose it and you might just lose the case.

5. Don't think about "where the questioner is going." If you do, you're not listening to the current question.

6. If you say something you shouldn't have, don't dwell on it. Doing so will cause you to make more mistakes.

7. Pause before you respond. It gives you think time, masks hesitancy, and gives your attorney time to object.

8. Listen to your attorney's objections. He or she may be trying to tell you something.

9. Never let yourself get hurried in a response. Take your time.

10. Once you complete your response to a question, stop talking. Don't let a stare from your questioner accompanied by a long silence cause you to say more.

CHAPTER TWELVE

Handling Crisis Communications

AT-A-GLANCE SUMMARY

This chapter is about effective communication in a crisis situation. Depending on the nature of your business, a crisis can take many different forms, but it's essential that you immediately recognize its onset.

Communications strategies must be in place and ready to be implemented *prior* to an actual crisis. Team planning, constituency targeting, media selection, and symbolic communication are all part of the mix in communicating your way through a crisis.

Finally, once a crisis ends, saying so, loudly and publicly, is a crucial element in getting things back on the road to normalcy.

"When you're up to your ass in alligators, it's difficult to remember that your original objective was to clean out the swamp." That old Southern adage is a handy summation of the need for effective crisis management and communication. The literature on crisis management will provide you with interesting accounts of how others have managed and survived crises. But ultimately, you're the expert on your own business and will use your expert knowledge to manage your way around and through a crisis.

What you may not do so well in a crisis situation is communicate. One of the main purposes of this chapter is to see that you don't ignore the communication function in the midst of a crisis, because how well you communicate with your public during a crisis will quickly become as important as your management of the crisis itself.

When survival, or finding a solution to the problems that precipitated the state of crisis, becomes your all-encompassing activity, such normal activities as communicating with your various constituents—customers, shareholders, the media, the general public, and regulatory agencies—can fall to a lower priority.

Once communication is put on the back burner, even if it seems absolutely necessary, all your various constituents are left to fend for themselves in figuring out what's going on. Irreparable damage may be done at this juncture, even if you manage your way out of the crisis itself. If the flow of information is stopped or severely stemmed, you or your organization will be considered inept, uncaring, secretive, or unethical, to some degree—perceptions that can be lethal in any business.

Identifying a Crisis

The definition of a crisis is clouded by the overuse of the term and the fact that we have become relatively accustomed to functioning in a so-called crisis situation with considerable normalcy.

As a long-time faculty member of the City University of New York, I am in a good position to point out that New York City has been in a state of continuing financial crisis for most, if not all, of my twenty years of service. Thus the mention of another squall in this continuing "crisis" must usually be accompanied by the admonition, "This time it's really serious," because things have come to the point where the word "crisis" has little impact.

A true crisis can take many forms, but it can essentially be defined as any situation that drastically and negatively affects your business to the extent that survival of the organization in its present state is imperiled.

In the banking business, a crisis can be an invisible but devastating failure to meet regulatory requirements and a loss of public confidence. In the automobile business, crisis can be a perceived design flaw that sends customers to competitors' showrooms, or a crippling recall and the bad publicity that goes with it. In the pharmaceutical industry, crisis can be a spate of deaths or injuries related to the use of a product. In other industries, the crisis may come in the form of an environmental accident or even a terrorist action or hostage situation. In any industry or organization, a sudden loss of or change in leadership can constitute a crisis.

History has proved on repeated occasions that corporations that are forthright and communicative in the midst of a crisis are the ones that survive and prosper, whereas those that stonewall, obfuscate, and engage in cover-ups either perish or spend vast amounts of time and resources in the struggle to survive.

Defining Your Specific Crisis

Even *before* a crisis happens, your goal should be to define just what constitutes a crisis, or specifically which situations or events could jeopardize or seriously disrupt your business. Here is a list of events that I would put in the crisis category and in need of crisis-specific communication:

- Environmental accidents
- Product failures involving a large number of units
- Product failures involving customer fatalities
- Hostage or hijacking situations
- Terrorist or sabotage situations
- Major litigation
- Severely negative media coverage
- Abrupt or controversial changes in senior management
- Bankruptcy filings or severe financial reversals

This list suggests a range of possibilities; using it as a starting point, develop an expanded list based on situations specific to your particular field. In this manner, you can develop a set of crisis-management plans and an equally important crisis-communications plan. The history of crisis management tells us that crises are usually foreseeable, and it is in this pre-crisis period that you should be setting up a communications plan.

Developing a Crisis-Communications Plan

The focus here is the establishment of a plan of action to be set in motion once a crisis occurs so that information will continue to flow to your constituents in an orderly and strategic manner. Of course, in planning for a crisis you will have developed a proposed strategy for dealing with the crisis itself, but the battlefield of crisis management is littered with the carcasses of companies whose management reacted astutely and decisively to the crisis yet failed to communicate any of their actions.

Select Your Crisis-Communications Team

Assembling the right team to execute your plan is as important as the plan itself. Your team should be organized in five areas:

1. External advisers
2. Internal advisers
3. Issues advisers
4. Legal advisers
5. Constituency managers

External Advisers

At the scene of a major fire, the chief or officer in command rarely, if ever, enters a burning building. The reasoning here is that the smoke-and-obstacle-filled inside of a burning building is a lousy place from which to view the fire and make effective command decisions.

Similarly, the middle of a crisis is a lousy place from which to see yourself as others see you. Yet this is just the perspective you need to manage crisis communications effectively.

This is what public-relations people do best; they don't just know your business, they know how your public feels about it and the job you are doing in running it. They can help you get your story out, decide which media to use, which audiences to concentrate on, and in what sequence—all details that may seem peripheral or frivolous when a crisis has you locked in a struggle for survival.

I am not suggesting that you listen to their every dictum. If you do, you're no longer in charge, and you should be. But if your organization is of sufficient size and consequence to affect and be affected by public opinion, hiring external public-relations advisers is a step you should consider long before the onset of a crisis. This way, when the issues climate heats up to the crisis stage, or even before, you have external advisers that you know and trust.

Internal Advisers

Here I am referring to your own internal public-affairs or public-relations people, who should be an integral part of your crisis-communications team. Depending on the role of this particular group within your organization, they can serve as spokespersons (often having relationships with local media that can be extremely helpful in a crisis period) or as liaisons with senior management for your external public-relations team.

Specifically defining these tasks prior to the crisis will enable the internal and external public-relations teams to work for *you* instead of against each other, which will certainly be the case if you start doling out power to a group of "Outsiders" in the midst of a crisis.

Plan on choosing between the advice of your legal team and your public-relations team. (They will usually differ.)

Perhaps it's a flaw inherent in both internal and external public-relations teams, especially in a crisis—even a flaw to which this writer is prone—but the advice of many public-relations types, boiled down to just a few words, will amount to, "Tell everyone everything, immediately."

Armed with a legal rather than a public-relations perspective, your lawyers are likely to give you advice that, when boiled down to its essence, amounts to, "Don't tell anyone anything, ever."

The lawyers earn their pay by telling you not to do things that will get you into difficulty, whereas public-relations people will pull you toward an active stance, communicatively speaking. Your job as a manager is to make a choice or seek a balance between these camps.

What your attorneys are concerned about, and often rightly so, is that a flurry of well-intentioned, forthright information on the nature and causes of a crisis, as well as what you are doing about it, will also contain admissions of what you may have done incorrectly, implying that you are in some way responsible for the crisis itself. You may also be blamed if your crisis management steps are not as effective as you thought they would be.

Lawyers have to worry about how your statements will play in court, whereas your public-relations advisers have to worry about how they will play in the court of public opinion.

I recently learned of an incident in which a customer was severely injured while using one of the company's products. The story received considerable media attention, focusing heavily on the impact of the victim's injury on his family.

Senior executives of the company decided to make a substantial cash contribution to the family in order to help with their immediate needs. The company's attorneys vigorously opposed this gesture, lest it be portrayed in subsequent legal actions as an admission of responsibility for the injury that occurred. Senior management in this case decided to ignore or at least set aside the advice of their legal team in favor of what they thought to be an appropriate gesture in spite of the possibility of adverse legal consequences.

Taking a purely legalistic stance may present you as a totally self-serving concern that places its balance sheet above the public interest. The history of corporations in crisis would suggest that those who relied excessively on legal advice may survive in the courts but not necessarily in the marketplace.

In summary, your legal advisers should be an important part of your crisis-communications team, to be relied on in avoiding or minimizing the legal consequences of your crisis. Also, the advice of your internal and external public-affairs teams may be in conflict.

The final decision about which advice to follow should be made on the basis of how important your legal position is compared with public perception of your product, service, or organization. Total legal success or exoneration from any blame in the causes or consequences of a crisis will be a hollow victory if gained at the expense of your reputation.

Issues Advisers

Issues advisers are the members of your crisis communications team who are there to give you specific information related to particular areas of your company's operations. Their specialties may range from customer relations to engineering to accounting and finance. The purpose of an issues adviser is to make certain that you get the latest and most accurate information on how a crisis is affecting your operations.

In assembling your team of issues advisers, reach down into the ranks and get the input of someone at the level of, let's say, an area manager. The usual tendency in a crisis is to choose the vice president of operations as your issues adviser for that area. Depending on company politics and culture, you may find that those who head entire divisions might be receiving a more positive spin on the operations picture (from their underlings) than someone who is closer to it on a daily basis.

Much has been made of GM's success in using a "team approach" to building its Saturn automobiles. If any worker sees a better way of doing things or has a suggestion on how to improve the product, he or she has immediate access to management. Workers also have greater autonomy in their "teams" in deciding the best way to accomplish a task.

The results of the team approach have been dramatic improvements in both product and productivity. Like so many great ideas, it was there all the time, just waiting for corporate culture to change enough to permit such flexibility. In assembling your team of crisis-issues advisers, cast a wide net, and the quality and accuracy of the internal information you need to handle the crisis will improve dramatically.

Constituency Managers

In the other chapters I have pointed out the importance of not ignoring the audience. In a crisis, getting the story out and managing and solving the crisis at the same time are often conflicting tasks. The problem is further compounded by the widely divergent needs of constituencies such as shareholders, customers, regulators, the media, and perhaps even victims and their families in cases involving death and injury. They all need to hear about the crisis and what you are doing about it, but they all have different perspectives.

The risk you run here is in either ignoring a group altogether or giving them the impression they are somehow less important than another of your constituencies. You can lessen the chance of doing damage to your relationships with any of these important groups by appointing a communicative adviser to represent the interests of each constituency.

As with the rest of the crisis-communications team, your various constituencies should be defined and a team put in place *before* there is any need to make use of them.

Identifying and Reaching Your Target Audience

Who needs to know what, and in what order should they be told? Not only do you need to define the audience in the absence of crisis, you must also determine priorities. It will be important to notify some constituents before others—your customers, bankers, shareholders, regulatory agencies, employees, unions, the general public.

If death or injuries are involved, you need to communicate with victims or their families.

Informing the wrong people, or the right people in the wrong order, is all too likely if you fail to determine your target audiences and sequence of communicating with them in advance.

Selecting the Appropriate Crisis-Communications Media

Once your crisis-communications team is assembled and you know who your audiences are and the sequence in which they should receive information, the next step is to develop a plan for reaching various segments of your audience. Following are some methods of communication you will want to review in assembling your communications plan.

Personal Contact

Particularly important players, perhaps board members or regulatory officials, should be contacted personally. If they first hear of your problem from a reporter, the consequences won't be positive. Once a crisis erupts you can be sure the media will be in touch with such parties for their reaction to your plight. *Before* you need it, draw up a list of the individuals to be contacted and designate who will make such calls should the need arise.

Executive-Employee Briefings

Handling a crisis situation always requires an extra measure of effort from employees. Don't expect heroic measures from people who have to learn what their company's management is doing by reading about it in the newspaper or seeing a senior executive on CNN.

The importance of internal communications in a crisis situation cannot be overstated. Remember that your employees become a primary source of information within the surrounding community during a crisis. An ill-informed staffer, or one who is hostile because he or she has been left "out of the loop" can do considerable damage, especially if happened upon by a reporter.

Formulate an internal-communications plan that includes communications from senior officials. When personal briefings are not feasible due to company size or a multiplicity of locations, consider a satellite television feed. Make internal communications, especially regularly scheduled employee briefings, a part of your communications plan.

Press Conferences

Hold them early and hold them often, or at least on a regular schedule. Except with proprietary information or legally problematic material, be open and communicative. Even if there are areas you can't talk about, tell those present exactly why you're not talking.

If you want the media off your back during a crisis, remember that the degree and kind of coverage you get after the initial flurry, in which you may be lead-story material, is in inverse proportion to your degree of accessibility. Your nearly constant willingness to share information on your actions in a crisis will ultimately reduce the degree of coverage you get. On the other hand, if the media sense any kind of cover-up, the story can simmer for months or even years. The most notorious political, corporate, and financial scandals that dot our history have given the field of crisis communication the mantra "It's not the crime, it's the cover-up!"

Reporters fancy themselves investigators, and once a story has been *completely* told (no more dirt to dig, or dirty laundry to air, or smoking gun to find), they are likely to fade from the scene. In fact, on a light-news day, such openness may even get you coverage on the high-quality job you're doing in getting your story across.

Hotlines

If you are in a business that involves a lot of customers and your product is one that could be dangerous if improperly used, if you have to give complicated directions, or if the situation or the nature of the crisis changes hourly, you may want to consider a hotline. This way customers, shareholders, reporters, or any portion of your constituency can get up-to-the-minute information.

Such telephone numbers are a common tool of the pharmaceutical industry to supply product information to patients as well as healthcare professionals. In the case of a product defect or recall, hotline numbers can be an extremely important tool, not just for providing vital information, but as reassurance to your public that you are sufficiently concerned about their well-being to provide this service.

If you decide to use a hotline as one of your crisis-communications tools, give careful consideration to how it is staffed and the method of communication—live and personal, or recorded.

This writer recommends against recorded messages as the sole voice on the hotline. In a crisis, recorded messages can also give the impression that everyone has jumped ship and a recording machine has been left to handle things. If staffing demands or the sheer volume of calls you expect make the use of a recorded message necessary, provide updates on a scheduled basis and make that schedule part of the message.

Special Mailings

Mailgrams, express letters, faxes, e-mail, and Web sites are effective ways to provide clarifications to important segments of your public. In crises requiring the communication of detailed information to a relatively sophisticated audience, an audience-tailored written message should be your choice.

Such mailings are particularly effective in supplying detailed financial, legal, or technical information that is not appropriate or feasible to deliver via the press conference or the sound byte.

One cautionary note: don't include information in a mailing that you don't want to see in the newspapers or on the air. Expect that information contained in a mailing to customers or stockholders or any large group will be leaked, intentionally or otherwise. The information should therefore be consistent with statements made in other forums, or you'll find yourself with a credibility crisis.

As to the specific content of a crisis mailing, you should include *your* version of the facts, a reason why the letter is being sent, and a definitive statement of what is being done about the crisis, as well as a timetable in which you will have the situation under control. Be certain to have the name of a real person on any communication. Letters signed "The Management" or even "The Executive Committee" have all the credibility of the line "You may have already won . . ."

Make sure that the special and urgent nature of the mailing is conveyed early in the message, perhaps even indicated on the outside of the envelope, but also remember that the importance of a piece of mail has been said to be in inverse proportion to the amount of printing on the outside of the envelope.

Print and Electronic Media Ads

If your audience is both numerically large and demographically diverse, and the crisis has received widespread media coverage, you may wish to consider media announcements—including print, radio, and television—to state your position and inform the general public about the crisis.

In constructing a newspaper ad, include, as you did in the direct-mail piece, a specific mention of those at whom the ad is aimed, the reason for the message (the crisis situation), what specific actions you are taking, and a timetable for getting things back to normal.

If you feel you have been wronged by the media in terms of the kind of coverage your crisis has received (and almost everyone does, both during and after a crisis), don't use your media announcements to attack the media. You'll appear defensive and embittered rather than in command of the situation. Also, various media may choose to respond by questioning both the accuracy of your position and your motivation in running the announcements. What started out as an attempt to communicate with the public and demonstrate your effectiveness as a manager becomes the basis for another round of unfavorable media coverage.

Who Is Your Spokesperson?

In a crisis the public will obviously want to know what you are doing to solve the problem; they'll also want to know about those in charge: whether they seem capable, trustworthy, decisive, and most of all, credible. This is why it is most important to have a senior executive as your chief spokesperson in a time of crisis.

While many complain about the undue influence of media, it is not the highly paid anchor people or hard-hitting investigative reporters who have the real clout and credibility in a crisis; it's the actual people in charge, those who make the decisions and take the actions, rather than just ask about and report on them.

A professional spokesperson or actor may deliver the message in the fewest "takes" and with the most fluency, but that professional spokesperson says nothing about who you are and what you're doing in this time of crisis. In fact, the use of a hired spokesperson may even suggest that you have something to hide (namely, your senior management). Having a professional spokesperson or actor deliver your media statement is equivalent to having a receptionist sign your annual message to the shareholders.

Making Use of Symbolic Communication

A vital and often neglected area of handling and communicating effectively in a crisis, symbolic communication refers to actions or messages of senior management clearly symbolizing that things are either under control or back to normal.

It's long been a tradition on the American political scene to engage in symbolic communication—for example, to have a President travel to an auto factory to deliver an address on the importance of buying

American or to a school to sign an important piece of education-related legislation. Such moments do more than provide photo opportunities for politicians. They also deliver a two-pronged symbolic message: first, that the issue was important enough to make this special trip, and second, to convey the impression that this executive is involved and has a hands-on approach. Such symbolic communication is especially important in effective crisis communication and should be included as part of your action plan.

Maintain Executive Visibility

An important symbol of how well a company is weathering a storm of crisis is the level of visibility of its senior management. If, at the outset of a crisis, senior management members are suddenly inaccessible and invisible, they will quickly gain an image not unlike that of Mafiosi seen in newscasts, darting out of courthouses with trench coats pulled over their heads.

Yes, in a crisis, you'll be busy, but don't become invisible. As a senior executive, if you find it necessary or desirable to appoint a spokesperson, personally introduce that spokesperson to the media in his or her first press conference. The gesture will lend that new voice some of your authority and credibility.

Don't Hide from the Troops

Another important area of symbolic communication is visibility to employees. Although, like most troops, they understand that the generals are not usually in the front lines, employees need the support and visibility of senior executives, especially in a time of crisis.

Remember that any time a crisis occurs—when an airliner crashes, when an automobile manufacturer issues a major recall—employees are out there taking the questions and sometimes the heat from almost everyone they encounter. At the same time, they may be expected to perform at heightened levels to get through the crisis period.

Don't Just Stand There Answering Questions—Do Something!

Another important type of symbolic communication lies in the actions you take as a senior executive in a crisis. Any gesture that says things are under control or are going to be okay soon is important in restoring public confidence. For example, if it is a product recall, showing footage of a product being removed from store shelves along with a statement of reassurance from a senior executive might be suitable. The point is to make it visible to the public that you are making a proactive response to the crisis.

Similarly, any message or gesture that says, "We're okay and so are our products" should be considered as soon as is feasible and credible during a crisis. If there is a question about a product, a personal message from the CEO or a demonstration of a product in use can be that important piece of symbolic communication that may be sought by your people.

Announce the END of the Crisis!

It Ain't Over till You Say It's Over

Crises have a lot in common with meteorologic catastrophes. Like hurricanes and blizzards, they can be predicted. Precautions can be taken, but even in the face of such measures, tremendous destruction can ensue. After a storm, the return to normalcy is often rapid. That very resumption of routine activity serves as a communal symbol that all is once again as it was. A corporate crisis may be well managed, and your management of the crisis may well have been successful, but often there are no striking visible symbols that things are back to normal unless you create them.

Therefore, once a crisis has passed, you should say so. Once your plants are up and running or at least the last repair or replacement of a defective product has been made, you should say so. Your media choices will be determined by how best to reach your various constituents, but regardless of how you do it, the announcement that things are back to normal and that preventive measures are in place must be made strongly and definitively.

Surviving and prospering beyond a crisis should be viewed as a triumph of an effective management team that is deserving of applause. It is also a time to send a loud and clear message to those more distant from the crisis that you are back and that perceptions of your company as an organization in peril are history rather than headlines.

Summary

Effective crisis communication is best achieved by defining what constitutes a crisis and having a communication plan in place before that crisis occurs.

Generally, a crisis is defined as any event that causes the sudden and catastrophic stoppage of an organization's primary activity or service. In the face of such catastrophe, failure to define in advance what constitutes a crisis in your organization and to prepare a communication plan can result in chaos when the crisis strikes. In that scenario, you'll be faced with the dual problems of managing not only the crisis but also the all-important internal and public perceptions of how things are being handled and whether that organization can or should survive. The resulting disorder leaves the public and the media to draw their own conclusions as to the scope and seriousness of the situation, which is not something you want. You want to be in charge.

During a crisis, you'll hear conflicting messages from your advisers. Lawyers will likely tell you to say as little as possible, while the public relations people will urge a statement nearing full disclosure. Of course, the ultimate response must take into consideration the nature of this particular crisis and its impact on the public, but the advance structuring of a balanced crisis communication team of legal, public relations and technical experts can help facilitate your organization's standard rules on what and how much to say.

Often, survival during organizational crisis rests on the symbolic value of executive visibility. Absence of a senior-level spokesperson will be interpreted as an ostrich-like approach to the crisis and will send the signal that the company is really in danger. Regularly scheduled briefings by a senior executive or other credible spokesperson are essential to create and sustain the perception that things are under control.

Once a solution is reached, it is essential to say just that: the crisis is over, things are back to normal, and steps have been taken to prevent a recurrence. And the single most important element in avoiding future disaster is a systematic communication plan, developed before it's needed.

Quick Review:
Handling Crisis Communications

1. Anticipate and define crises before they happen.

2. Plan crisis-communication strategies in advance.

3. Maintain contact with the media at regular intervals if appropriate.

4. Have internal and external advisers as part of your communications team.

5. Decide in advance exactly who should be informed of a crisis and in what order.

6. Don't be afraid to call a crisis a crisis.

7. Plan your symbolic-communications strategies.

8. Keep your senior executives visible.

9. Talk to your employees early and often.

10. Once the crisis is over, say so.

CHAPTER THIRTEEN

Conducting Successful Meetings

AT-A-GLANCE SUMMARY

This chapter shows you how to conduct successful meetings and send the most positive signals about your leadership skills. It includes strategies to increase your level of effectiveness in running meetings, from arranging the meeting itself to managing the group dynamics and the characters that surface in any gathering of colleagues.

Often considered a necessary evil of corporate life, meetings are a way of getting decisions made and policies set; they may get things done, but few of us like attending them.

Newer members of an organization can feel that their input is unwelcome (and they may be correct), whereas senior executives may feel that the same decisions could be made in a flash without all this wasted time and input from subordinates (and they may also be correct).

Those in the middle will often use meetings as launching pads for their own agendas, constructive or otherwise, and will test the water with various levels of disagreement or confrontation. Some will attempt to operate within the agenda and try to get things done so that the meeting is not a waste of time.

All these behaviors and approaches to meetings are, in reality, power struggles. Some attempt to gain power by manipulating the agenda, and others show their distaste for power or, more correctly, those in power, by not participating. Even those who do participate may be doing so only to seek recognition of those in charge.

As a manager, you can have a masterful grasp of the most complex nuances of your field, but if your meeting-management skills are not what they should be, you will be alternately accused of being a bully, a wimp, a tyrant, a nitpicker, or a bumbling generalist. If you are consistently ineffective in running meetings, that failing will be generalized to other areas of your performance.

Your effectiveness in handling meetings will shape the perception of your overall effectiveness as a leader: how you handle the ebb and flow of agreement and conflict, as well as the interaction of varying personalities; and whether you get things done or the meeting ends up in ideational disarray. If you follow the steps outlined here, people may not look forward to coming to your meetings but you will get more done in less time and reduce conflict.

Using an Agenda to Establish and Maintain Control

"You're probably wondering why I called you here" is a disastrous meeting opener. It says to those gathered that you're secretive, and they will spend part of the time wondering what you're up to rather than listening to what you have to say. Agendas should be distributed in advance, in order to give the participants time to formulate their own ideas on the agenda items.

An agenda enhances control and productivity for a meeting in several ways. First of all, those in attendance have expectations of what is to be discussed and will usually come prepared, not just with the required materials, but also with ideas generated by an advance look at your agenda.

Agendas also help set the tone of the meeting. For example, if a meeting agenda has a wide variety of items for discussion, it can serve as an indication that there is a lot to be done and those in attendance should be prepared for a busy session. In contrast, if an item of extreme importance is under consideration, having it as the sole agenda item or presenting an unusually brief agenda sends a clear signal to participants that the meeting is of particular importance.

Finally, agendas present a structure that in more formal settings permit you as leader, or even permit participants, to make sure a meeting moves forward by prohibiting the discussion of items that are not on the agenda. (See the section on selecting a level of formality in this chapter.) Once again, depending on the level of formality and the culture in which the meeting is being held, prohibition of discussion of nonagenda items in a politely insistent manner will ensure that meetings cover *exactly* the items or areas intended.

Before continuing, it is important to note that there are two types of gatherings that are often confused with meetings: so-called brainstorming sessions and therapy sessions. In the former, those present may be asked to focus on an issue or problem and work together on developing new approaches to the matter under consideration. In the latter, one may freely discuss a problem on a random or even chaotic path to an informational destination.

Obviously, brainstorming and therapy sessions have their place in the search for solutions, but they are generally unfettered by deadlines or budgetary restraints. Also, unlike traditional meetings, the lack of forward motion is not considered a failure, but merely an indication of the need for further brainstorming or therapy. The meetings considered in this chapter are strictly of the variety requiring that things get done on time with a minimum of upheaval—meetings at which the lack of results indicates failure rather than the need for more meetings.

You may want to structure meetings with the following categories as a guide for your agenda:

1. Reading of the minutes (or statement of purpose and definition of a newly convened group)
2. Approval of the minutes from the previous meeting (which have been distributed in advance of the meeting with enough time for those present to have reviewed them)

3. Old business, considering unfinished items or tabled motions from the previous meetings

4. New business (agenda items submitted)

5. Elections, if required; the establishment of election procedures should be included as an early agenda item in newly convened groups

Using the basic items as building blocks, you should be able to construct an agenda for a newly established body, or reshape and systematize the agenda for a group in need of reorganization.

A cautionary note: don't edit an agenda to avoid discussing issues or to manipulate a group; you will only make people distrustful and noncommunicative. In planning an agenda, the objective should be to get business done efficiently.

Encouraging Participant Input

An effective way to gain input without giving up control of the agenda is to establish a policy that staff members will be allotted a portion of the meeting time for items they wish to discuss. This makes it clear that input is welcome and planned. The purposefulness and sincerity of staff communication will be increased, and control of the agenda can be preserved. Don't fear loud meetings, flying feathers and all, as long as the items discussed are on the agenda.

Establishing a Regular Meeting Schedule

If you are a new manager and your company doesn't already have a meeting schedule and a mechanism for gathering agenda items, establish them. As the one who institutes this policy, you will have communicated that you want input and that you intend to seek it in an organized, systematic manner. This gesture also communicates that you are organized, in charge, and yet willing to listen.

Regularly scheduled meetings can always be canceled if circumstances dictate, but the presence of that regular meeting on a schedule tells employees that there will be an opportunity for discussion on a regular basis, an important escape valve in the presence of problems.

Begin on Time

Employees, like the schoolchildren they once were, will test the corporate culture on the starting time of meetings. A 2:00 p.m. time can quickly degenerate to 2:10 and beyond if you let it. Exert your authority and always begin within five minutes of the scheduled starting time, even if all those expected have not yet arrived. You thus indicate that you are there to get things done and are in charge not only of the schedule, but the group itself.

I recognize that what I've just said may be a bit harsh in less formal environments or when the atmosphere is more relaxed; you might consider building in a kind of time cushion such as "coffee and . . . will be served at 2:00 p.m. with the meeting to begin promptly at 2:15." You've said that the meeting will begin promptly, but in a kinder, gentler way. You've communicated the same no-nonsense, let's-get-down-to-business attitude, but you've humanized it by saying "relax and have some coffee first."

End on Time

Meetings with a definite concluding time are those at which the most is accomplished. Why? It's not only the pressure of the clock that makes us work harder. (Who was it who said, "The amount of time a task takes is proportional to the amount of time available to complete the task"?) It's also the absence of the feeling that "this thing will go on forever" that makes a meeting more bearable, especially for those with tight schedules.

If you schedule a meeting with a predetermined ending time, you are communicating not only your own sense of organization, but consideration of other people's schedules. The trade-off is that you'll find those present are willing to work harder and more constructively, rather than feeling they are unwilling guests in *The Twilight Zone* in an episode entitled, "The Endless Meeting."

Planning for the Effective Meeting

A major key to successful meetings is proper advance planning, particularly with regard to items that cannot and should not be decided during a meeting.

Select an Appropriate Level of Formality

"Move to table the motion. Is the motion seconded? All in favor of the motion signify by saying aye." The chairperson of a meeting stands at the podium, rattling off parliamentary rules with the rapidity and dispassion of an auctioneer, changing the direction, the length, and even the outcome. This is the stuff of parliamentary procedure, so named because of the origins of such rules in the British Parliament, as outlined in *Robert's Rules of Order.*[3]

How should you proceed, formally or informally? The corporate culture and expectations of those who attend a meeting will greatly shape the level of formality that will be tolerated. *Robert's Rules,* no rules, or somewhere in between? The choice you make should be based on four factors:

1. The size of the group
2. The atmosphere of the meeting
3. The degree of importance of the meeting
4. Your degree of knowledge of and experience
   with parliamentary procedure

---

3. Marjorie Mitchell Carr, *Robert's Rules of Order—Simplified* (New York: Perigee Books, 1991).

Informal meetings should be the rule with fewer than ten people in the room. In a group this size, everyone will generally know everyone else, and in this informal atmosphere, there is no need to start applying rules that can cut off discussion, cause division, and seem to stifle opposing points of view for being "out of order."

The resentment caused by such rules in an informal setting, or their sudden or inconsistent application, will be viewed with suspicion and justified resentment and will not be worth the time saved.

Once a group has more than ten or twelve members, however, permitting everyone equal access to debate the issue at hand or trying to gain consensus rather than election becomes too cumbersome and time consuming. If rules are introduced for the purpose of improving the flow and productivity of the meeting rather than to control or stifle the exchange of ideas, they are generally welcomed.

Understand the Legal Consequences of Your Meetings

You'll need to examine the work of the group you are presiding over in the context of how important that group's work is from a legal point of view.

Are your decisions going to be subject to subsequent review, perhaps in a court of law? Will there be questions about how decisions were arrived at and whether the rules were consistently applied?

If your answers to these questions are in the affirmative, regardless of the group's size, you'll want to adopt a set of rules and stick by them. You should also check with your legal counsel before getting started, to avoid potentially serious errors if your work is to be reviewed or might face challenges from external entities.

Study the Rules before You Get to the Meeting

The effective application of rules designed to keep an agenda on track, limit debate, and carry out elections in an orderly and just manner requires knowledge of the rules and experience in applying them. You'll need to use a dual level of attention, not only to the items under discussion, but also to how they are in compliance or violation of the rules for the meeting (such as whether an item of discussion should be ruled irrelevant or "out of order," as is said in meeting parlance).

Get Help if You Need It

If you are not that experienced in chairing meetings and you intend to run a meeting under strict parliamentary rules, give strong consideration to appointing a parliamentarian and keep a copy of *Robert's Rules* or some similar guide on hand. This way you can maintain compliance with a set of meeting rules while you focus on the issues at hand.

Keeping the Peace at Meetings

If certain decisions are not made in advance of meetings, making them during a meeting will be perceived as manipulation rather than effective management and could create a level of resentment that will be difficult to reverse. Here are some preventive strategies that should improve the meeting atmosphere.

Define the Group

If matters are to be decided by vote, the group should be defined in terms of exactly who the eligible voters are. For example, members of a task force or committee may have a full vote, but what about their support staff, who may be present at the meeting? If not decided in advance, and if everyone votes, you may wind up with a classic case of the tail wagging the dog if the support staff or part-time members of the group constitute a majority.

Define a Majority

What should be decided by a simple majority and what by two-thirds vote? Should the electorate be defined as all the members of a given group, or just those present at the meeting? What about absentee voting—should it be permitted? Can those who were not present and did not hear the discussion cast an informed vote?

Your decisions on these seemingly simple questions can drastically affect the outcome of a group's work. All these questions need to be answered at the beginning of your work, if your meetings will make decisions by casting votes. Attempting to make decisions about voter eligibility in the presence of issues and likely outcomes looks like manipulation and probably is. Set your electoral rules before you consider any other issues.

Don't Let a Meeting Degenerate into a Gripe Session

A meeting is normally a time to form consensus, provide information, or develop policy in handling an issue or problem. However, if morale in an organization is low, or if meetings in the past have been too few and far between, meetings can easily and inadvertently become forums for people to vent their anger, outrage, or whatever other negative emotion is in the air. Once the atmosphere at a meeting becomes charged with such negativity, it can be difficult to get things back on track. As the one who presides, you may be seen as a part of the problem rather than the solution if your meetings become the major forum to air complaints.

If there is a morale problem or a number of negative or potentially negative situations that require discussion, consider setting up a separate meeting billed strictly as a gripe session or a forum in which complaints can be aired. You may wish to label such meetings as "gripe sessions," "town meetings," or even "verbal suggestion boxes." No matter what you call them, keep these meetings focused on the problem issue and differentiate them from your regularly scheduled meetings.

Having a separate meeting to air complaints will demonstrate that you care about your employees' problems and their solutions, while preserving the integrity, structure, and purpose of a meeting held to conduct company business. You can also place agenda items of a "gripe" nature on the "gripe-session" agenda, thus ensuring that regular meetings can remain task or accomplishment oriented.

Don't Overuse the "Emergency Meeting" Designation

The designation "emergency meeting" should be reserved for such occasions when a *real* crisis comes up and attendance is absolutely essential.

One department manager I know was in the habit of designating practically every meeting he held as an "emergency meeting." His memoranda were usually laced with the word "crisis." This manager was communicating to his personnel that he viewed everything as a crisis; more than one of his staffers would say he was from the "Chicken Little" school of managers.

Use the words "crisis" and "emergency" sparingly in referring to your meetings. Thus, when a serious problem needs to be tackled, you'll get help and cooperation rather than a behind-your-back shrug that says: "There he (or she) goes again."

Once the Meeting Begins

Calling for a Quorum

A quorum is defined in *Robert's Rules* as the majority of all members. Therefore, in order to conduct business fairly, especially when matters are being voted on, a quorum should be present. In fact, *Robert's Rules* further states that business conducted in the absence of a quorum is "null and void."

While it is traditionally the duty of a chairperson to monitor the number present, any member of the group can, as is said in meeting parlance, "call for a quorum." Once a quorum has been called, the business of the meeting is halted and the number of voting members is counted. If the number of those present is less than the defined majority of eligible voters, the only business to be discussed is that of an adjournment time, with all other business suspended.

Practicality sometimes dictates that this rule be suspended, which is done formally by a majority vote of those present. If the group agrees, then business can continue, with all actions taken to be ratified at a subsequent meeting at which a quorum is present. Given the reality of conflicting schedules and priorities, suspending a quorum can be a highly practical measure. When crucial matters are under deliberation and being voted on, however, conducting substantive business without a quorum can be unfair and leave you on legally shaky ground.

Maintaining Order

No, this is not a few words about alternative uses of a gavel, but clearly one of your jobs is to keep the meeting running smoothly, and a major component of this task is to keep the discussion orderly and on target. You should inform the group *at the outset* that members are to speak when recognized by the chairperson and that extraneous or "off the point" discussion or comments will be ruled out of order and not permitted to continue.

The application of such rules should be consistent and should be intended only to advance the smooth and expeditious running of the meeting, rather than the advancement of the chair's favored causes. A chair who attempts to manipulate these rules will quickly manipulate himself or herself out of all personal credibility and authority. Be careful!

Making and Seconding of Motions and Discussion

A motion or recommendation that an action be taken should be seconded. Motions are generally accepted only from voting members of a group and must be seconded by another voting member of the group before discussion can begin. If the motion is not seconded, it is an indication that there is no other interest in discussing the motion, and no further consideration is given it, or, as they say in parliamentary terms, the motion "dies."

If the motion is seconded, the chair then calls for discussion on the motion just seconded. During that discussion, your function as chair is to recognize those who have comments on the motion, interrupting and stopping that discussion as being "out of order" if it does not pertain specifically to the motion that has been seconded or is "on the floor."

Point of Order or Information

During a meeting, someone may spot a flaw in the procedures being followed. Perhaps a motion was not seconded or a comment is on something other than the motion being discussed. In such cases, any member may call for a "point of order" or an immediate ruling from the chair on the perceived procedural irregularity.

Similarly, a "point of information" is a request for information, often clarification of a motion under discussion or about to be voted on. Points of order and information generally receive immediate recognition from the chair on the assumption that if they are not cleared up promptly, proper procedure cannot be maintained and fully informed discussion or voting cannot take place.

Voting or "Calling the Question"

Once everyone who wishes to speak on an issue has been heard, the chair may call for a vote by simply asking if the group is ready to vote on the motion and proceeding with the vote in the absence of any negative response.

In a larger group, or when greater formality is preferable, you may want to have the group vote on whether they wish to vote on the motion under discussion immediately or continue discussion. This is known as a vote to "call the question." If the vote (by show of hands or ballot) to call the question fails, discussion of the motion is simply continued. If the vote to call the question is successful, the motion is then immediately voted on without further discussion.

Motions to call the question come from the floor and, like any other motion, must be seconded. Motions to call the question are usually deliberate attempts either to limit discussion or to shorten the meeting by expediting the voting process.

If discussion becomes repetitive, you may want to encourage such motions by asking if anyone present would like to make a motion to call the question. But once again, in a less formal setting, you might want to simply ask if the group is ready to vote.

Though it may be fairly obvious, it should be stated that the orderly running of a meeting necessitates that there only be one motion on the floor at a time and that no other motions be accepted for consideration until the one under consideration is voted on and passed or defeated.

Amending a Motion

Sometimes a motion is near passage but may have a flaw in wording or structure that is a problem to those who are about to vote on it. For example, there may be a motion on the floor that says: "The executive committee will meet monthly to review overtime costs as compared to productivity figures." Let's say that union members want some input at these meetings and, as nonmembers of the executive committee, are opposing this motion.

The motion can be amended by a voting member if the maker of the motion is willing to accept that change as part of the newly amended motion. For example, the amended motion may read as follows: "The executive committee will meet monthly to review overtime costs as compared to productivity figures. Two members of the union's steering committee may attend this meeting as nonvoting members at their option."

This would be considered a "friendly amendment." In the event the maker of the motion is unwilling to accept the amendment as a part of the motion, which is at his or her discretion, that motion is then to be voted on in its original form.

Record and Read the Motion

If your meeting is formal enough to require even a modified form of parliamentary procedure, it will be desirable to have a secretary present who is responsible for taking minutes. Another important function of that secretary is to write down the *exact* wording of a motion and read it to those present before voting takes place.

Especially when the outcome of a vote on a motion might have serious consequences, it is essential to the integrity of the deliberative process that the electorate have a *precise* awareness of just what they are voting on.

Often a motion is made, seconded, and followed by such extensive discussion that many of those present forget the contents altogether, or only retain a confused idea of the motion. In the interest of clarity and to avoid the extreme disarray and finger pointing that will result if people don't fully understand what they have voted for or against, always read the motion just before the vote takes place. Also be willing to repeat the motion as necessary.

Tabling the Motion

When a motion is under discussion and that discussion generates additional issues, or when the discussion reveals the need for further information that is not readily available, it may be time for someone to move that the motion be "tabled" or discussion be postponed.

Motions to table generally require seconding and a majority vote of those present for passage. Motions for tabling are not debatable, as such debate would defeat the purpose of the motion itself.

So that the motion to table will be viewed as a means of postponing action until a time when it can actually be accomplished rather than a means of avoiding the issue altogether, it is generally wise to include, in your motion to table, a definite time at which the motion will be taken up again, for example: "I move to table the motion until the quarterly figures are available for inclusion, with discussion to take place no later than the meeting on March 14."

Handling Confidential Information

If you are having a meeting on a confidential or proprietary matter, be certain to begin and end the meeting with a reminder of the confidential nature of the meeting and, when possible and applicable, the consequences attached to revealing information about the meeting. Your chances of keeping leaks of confidential information are increased by keeping the meeting as small as possible, but remember the words of Ben Franklin, who opined that there is absolutely no problem for three people to keep a secret—if two of them are dead.

Making Meetings More Efficient (aka *Shorter!*)

Before continuing on this topic, as a believer in full discussion and open communications, I should point out that there are times when a discussion has gone on too long and has become repetitive, overly heated, or even trivial. At such times, as the chair of the meeting, or as one of the participants, you may wish to consider the following perfectly acceptable strategies for limiting discussion, or even ending the meeting.

Limit Discussion Time

A time limit is a simple device that usually occurs to people when it's too late; discussion time on motions or agenda items should be decided on by vote *at the beginning* of a meeting before any discussion has taken place. This way no one will feel singled out by this restriction as they would if you attempted to introduce it at midmeeting. Depending on the complexity of the matter under discussion, you may wish to set the limit at anywhere from five minutes to even thirty minutes (someone should keep time), after which a vote should take place. Such limits are especially useful when you are under severe time constraints.

Motion to Adjourn

Once the business of the agenda is completed, there may be additional legitimate business. However, sometimes a few people are present who actually like meetings, or at least like making them longer than they need to be.

Meetings will often be adjourned simply by the clock or by people getting up to leave. As chair, you may wish to expedite things by asking for a motion to adjourn. Especially in handling the filibusterer, the motion to adjourn comes in very handy. Motions to adjourn are not debatable and will end the meeting with a majority vote of those present.

Voting and Secrecy

Be Willing to Use Secret Ballots

This is a courtesy those present will appreciate. Many meetings, particularly the more informal ones, rely on a simple show of hands for voting purposes.

If sensitive issues are being decided, you may wish to use a secret ballot, even in a small group. It's been my rule over the years to try to anticipate when sensitive issues would be under consideration and simply announce that voting for this particular meeting will be by secret ballot. This way confidentiality is ensured without becoming an issue.

At other times I have made it clear that if anyone present requested a secret ballot on any issue, the request would be granted without vote or deliberation. In this manner everyone's privacy is protected with a minimum of bother.

If you expect a request for a secret ballot, you'll need to have ballots at the ready. When voter anonymity is a particular necessity, you may even wish to have pencils or special pens available for the vote.

Set a Policy about Minutes and Other Forms of Recording

Minutes are generally a good idea as a record of what went on at prior meetings, not only to refresh the memories of those present at the previous session of the group, but also to provide orientation for those who may be new and for whom a sense of history of the group is required.

Following are samples of the various styles of minutes and some questions that should be answered as you decide which style best suits your purposes.

Detailed Summary Minutes

Resembling a court record, detailed summary minutes contain complete descriptions of what was said and by whom.

Here is a sample of how detailed summary minutes might look:

> The meeting began at 2:30 p.m. The first item of business was a report on the lawsuit against the Compton City Zoning Board headed by Gordon Pruett, vice-president for legal affairs. Mr. Pruett, in his summary, suggested the possibility of collusion between the realtor and the city council in denying the permit and pointed out that . . .

Action or Subject Outline Minutes

These are minutes that contain only a listing or brief summary of the items discussed without direct quotes or paraphrases of statements made. Here is a sample of action or subject outline minutes:

> The meeting began at 2:30 p.m. with a report on the legal action against the Compton City Zoning Board. Obstacles to the progress of the suit were summarized.

Whether to use a detailed or summary form of minutes should be decided on two bases. First, if there is a frequent turnover in the attendance at regularly scheduled meetings, detailed minutes will be helpful in keeping those who read them informed of the proceedings and better able to join the proceedings "in progress." A second consideration in whether to have detailed minutes and whether to include the names of those who speak during a meeting is the question of what happens to the minutes of the meeting. Are they widely circulated? Might the meeting be a forum where proprietary information is discussed? What about the legal or public-relations consequences of an inadvertent or even deliberate leak of information contained in the minutes? A look at the issues climate and nature of your business should enable you to reach a quick decision on the degree of detail you consider necessary in meeting minutes.

To Record or Not to Record

The quality and accessibility of recording equipment is much better than it was just a decade or two ago, with both audio and video recording prevalent in most of our nation's courtrooms.

However, as in the case of detailed meeting minutes, you should examine the consequences of making a video or audio record of the proceedings. The presence of cameras or microphones is likely to scare many away from the frank discussion that is often an important part of getting things done.

This is not to imply that recordings should therefore be made without the knowledge of those present. Recording people without their knowledge is always a breach of etiquette and quite possibly a breach of law. If you are recording, make certain that those being recorded know about it, and check with your legal counsel before making recording a business practice, in or out of meetings.

There is also the question of how important it is to have an *exact* record of the proceedings. Like putting too many things in writing, having a record as specific as an audio or video recording can come back to haunt you or others present.

In summary, while I'm providing you with options, I remain a fan of open, no-holds-barred, and even loud-discussion meetings, recorded in the form of brief summary minutes. I also believe in giving meeting participants the right to go on and off the record, or to have their comments appear in the minutes free of attribution.

A by-product of the freedom of operating under these rules is frank discussion of ideas in an atmosphere in which everyone will participate fully and openly, secure in the knowledge that it won't come back to haunt them.

Summary

Prepare for meetings by boning up on your parliamentary procedure and the meeting management techniques discussed in this chapter. But above all, encourage frank, free-flowing, and open discussion; show that you welcome it and listen to the participants' ideas and even challenges. You'll learn from them.

Use parliamentary procedure judiciously and always fight the clock, not the people in the room; your meetings will improve in tone, atmosphere, and level of accomplishment. *Is there a motion to adjourn?*

Quick Review:
Conducting Successful Meetings

1. Set an agenda and stick to it.

2. Hold regularly scheduled meetings.

3. Place time limits on all meetings.

4. Begin and end on time.

5. Don't let meetings become gripe sessions.

6. Don't overuse the designation "emergency meeting."

7. Define membership in the group and voting procedures before you get into issues.

8. Always be open to using secret ballots for elections.

9. Make an early decision about the degree of detail contained in meeting minutes.

10. Use parliamentary procedure to fight the clock, not the people in the room.

For More Information

Cann, Marjorie Mitchell. *Robert's Rules of Order—Simplified.* New York: Perigee Books, 1991.

Robert, Henry M. *The New Robert's Rules of Order.* Revised edition by Mary A. De Vries. New York: New American Library, 1990.

CHAPTER FOURTEEN

Twenty-Seven Quick Fixes to Improve Your Communicative Power

AT-A-GLANCE SUMMARY

The previous chapters have taken you from the speaker's podium to the TV studio, and even into the courtroom, providing you with suggestions, techniques, and tips. Some of them take more time to implement fully than others, particularly those that require practice or a change in your way of thinking.

This chapter is intended as a review of the most easily implemented tactics and techniques. Their use leads to immediate improvement in your communicative power and impact in a wide array of situations.

At the Podium

1. *Start your speeches with silence.* Whenever you approach a podium, some members of the audience will be talking among themselves or otherwise not paying attention. If you begin right away, sure, they'll gradually tune in, but they'll also be thinking about that prior conversation and not really listening to you. Talking over the noise also suggests that you're nervous, afraid of silence. Instead, after you approach the podium and arrange your notes, *don't speak,* but wait ten or even fifteen seconds. At this point, everyone will be listening and the attention will be focused on you and your message instead of whatever was going on before you began speaking.

2. *Don't waste the first few seconds.* Most speakers walk up to the podium, place their notes on it, adjust the microphone, and then utter the ridiculously redundant and totally boring words, "Today

I'm going to talk to you about . . ." It is perfectly obvious you are going talk about something even before you say anything. Don't waste that opening moment. It may the last time during your speech that everyone is paying attention, so say something that will grab and hold their attention. Even if it's controversial, at least they're listening.

3. *Always mention your audience specifically.* Public speaking is less intimate than conversation; speeches often take on the generic and impersonal quality of a government brochure. To make the audience feel "You're really talking to *us*," mention your audience by name, or even mention specific audience members. "Everyone knows that the federal budget is . . ." becomes, "As CPAs, you especially know that the federal budget is . . ."; "Many of you" becomes "From Alice in the Legal Department to Mary Kay in Public Affairs . . ." Even if you're giving the same speech a number of times, this small language adjustment keeps it fresh and increases listenership.

4. *Once you conclude, stop talking.* As I point out in Chapter 4 (the speechwriting chapter), you should begin the end of your speech with a concluding transitional phrase, for example, "In conclusion," or "To summarize." Most speakers seem to know this, but too many will use one of these closing phrases and then drone on for five or ten minutes. Once you indicate you're wrapping things up, never talk for more than two additional minutes; to do so is to lose all of your audience's attention and some of your credibility.

About the Words You Use

5. *Simpler is better.* Without talking down to an audience, use terms with which they are all familiar and define any that are in doubt. If you use acronyms or abbreviations, explain them at first mention if there is any possibility that someone present might not follow you. Speakers who say of an audience, "They'll figure it out," are correct—but while they're figuring, they're not listening.

6. *Name names.* Forgetting to mention your company name is an amusing and sometimes revealing error. In the dozens of hours that make up your work week, you may never have any reason to mention it at all. The problem occurs when you maintain this internal mind-set while speaking to an external audience. They don't know you and need to be reminded who you and your organization are. The error of leaving out the company name also shows up when a negative issue needs to be discussed publicly. In a lame attempt to disassociate themselves and their organization from whatever is going on, many spokespersons will all too conveniently omit the company name. This error, even if it's subconscious, makes you look like the little kid who missed the school bus and says, in a blame-shifting statement, "The bus left me behind."

7. *Watch your pronouns.* English is a sexist language in that it generally reflects, and some would say perpetuates, the male-dominated nature of the corporate and professional world. The feminists among us are distracted, if not offended, by the exclusion of female pronouns, particularly when referring to positions of power, expertise, or authority. So such sentences as, "Talk to any expert and he will say . . ." are a surefire way to offend the more socially aware members of your audience. Talk to any expert and just listen to what *he* or *she* has to say.

Handling Audience Questions

8. *Never say, "I'm glad you asked me that question."* No one believes you; they know you'd rather not be answering their questions at all. The same is true of that other equally ineffective stall used by many speakers, "That's a good question." Instead, pause before responding and, if you must stall for time, try saying something like, "You've raised a very important issue."

9. *If you don't know the answer to a question, say so.* Many speakers fear they'll be asked a question to which they don't know the answer. Actually, no audience expects you to know everything about any subject. "I don't know, but I'll find out," or "I don't know but let me tell you

who does," are answers that will do nothing to reduce your stature. And besides, once you've said, "I don't know," and you're being truthful, no one can argue with you.

10. *Don't look at a Q&A session as a battle to be won.* Instead, look at it as an information-sharing session in which you are likely to have to talk about some problem issues. Trying to win or weasel your way out of the tough questions will only leave the impression that you're defensive and embattled rather than informative and in charge.

In the Job Interview

11. *Prepare for the "Tell me about yourself" question.* It's always there. It's usually at the beginning and sets the tone for the entire interview. Because it's so obvious and deceptively simple, many interview subjects fail to anticipate this question and turn in a fumbled, poorly structured response.

12. *Decide what your strong points are and don't be modest in discussing them.* A job interview is a self-sales presentation, and success in sales presentations or job interviews does not go to the meek. Focus on a couple of strong points that relate to the job for which you're being interviewed and practice working these points into your responses.

13. *Know more about the company than the other candidates do.* Achieving a positive outcome in a job interview is often a matter of differentiating yourself from the competition. One relatively easy way to do so is to read such publications as the annual report, employee newsletter, and even recent news items. (This doesn't mean reading them in the reception area as you wait for the interview to begin.)

Most candidates don't know as much as they should about the problems and objectives of their prospective employer. Doing some homework here will separate you from the crowd.

In the Sales Presentation

14. *Don't be ashamed to sell.* You don't need me to tell you that selling is tough, especially because of the frequent rejection that's part of the job.

In selling, you quickly learn that most presentations go well and most prospects are awfully polite (they seldom reject you to your face). You also learn that most encounters result in no positive outcome or sale.

This reality may turn you into a member of those hordes of so-called sales professionals who approach prospects with the "I'm sorry to take up your time, but I'll be brief and let you go back to work" strategy. If you ever hear yourself saying words such as these or thinking such thoughts, you too have begun to substitute apologizing for selling. Don't apologize, sell! Take up their time with your presentation and make it worthwhile.

If you are there to sell and want to close that day, say so and work toward that *exact* goal. You'll make more sales by selling than by apologizing.

15. *Plan on coming back.* The rejection that is an inevitable part of selling means it may take more than one shot to succeed. Sometimes, even before you enter the room, they've decided to go with another vendor—despite your super, all-cylinders-clicking, all-barrels-blazing presentation. In light of this possibility, a secondary objective of your sales presentation should be to be invited back. This means being careful about knocking the competition and not making your prospect nervous or defensive about going with another vendor. Accentuate positives, tread lightly over the competition's negatives, and be invited back.

In the Media Interview

16. *Have an informational goal or a set of target issues for any media interview.* Prior to many media interviews I've conducted, I've said to guests, "What would you like to talk about?" Many respond by saying, "Anything you'd like." This is a mistake, especially if the interview is potentially adversarial. You should always try to anticipate and control the subject areas covered in media interviews, either by planning to mention some target issues or by being directive when asked the pre-interview question, "What would you like to talk about?"

17. *Remember, you are the expert—they are not.* Most reporters have somewhere between a surface idea and no knowledge at all about your interview subject. Yet even the foremost experts tend to be intimidated in the presence of reporters, answering unfair or ill-constructed questions in the hope that the reporter will "go easy." If there is something wrong with a question or you just don't understand it, politely say so and get yourself a better question or an admission that the reporter is merely fishing. Remember, *you* are the expert.

18. *Never say "No comment" to a reporter.* Sometimes you are asked a question you shouldn't answer. You might think a quick solution is to say "No comment!" A reporter's audience views that statement much the way people erroneously view taking the Fifth Amendment: you've got something to hide and you're probably guilty. Instead of saying "No comment!" tell the reporter why you won't be responding to a question. "It's proprietary information," "It's a matter to be decided in court, not here and now," or "I don't have sufficient information to make an intelligent comment" are all ways to say "No comment" without actually using those unintentionally incriminating words.

Conducting Meetings

19. *Use agendas for meetings and stick with them.* An important part of your perceived effectiveness in running meetings is the orderliness with which things proceed. Most of us remember to generate and distribute an agenda, but many fall short on sticking to it. Especially if you're just beginning a leadership role, you'll find that any group will test your willingness to be led away from your planned agenda. Sticking with that agenda, except under the most extreme circumstances, will get you through that test with your leadership skills intact.

20. *Begin meetings on time.* Another test you'll face, particularly in the early stages of a leadership role, is the tendency of groups to push back the starting time of meetings with tardy entrances. Once such patterns become the accepted routine, meetings can be delayed and

efficiency greatly undermined. By beginning at or very close to the scheduled time, you send a signal that there is work to be done and that it will be done even in the absence of those who are overly lax about starting times. Ending meetings on time is an important symbolic communication that you are as considerate of the participants' time as they have been of yours. Besides, little or no business is conducted when everyone in the room has somewhere else to go and can't get there because your meeting is running late. Once you've established a reputation for getting things done in the allotted time, you'll find the atmosphere more conducive to accomplishment and a positive commentary on your leadership skills.

21. *Don't let meetings become gripe sessions.* The chronic complainers in your midst can use a meeting as a platform to air their complaints. This behavior can snowball to the extent that your meetings are not directed toward productive ends, but instead become verbal dumping grounds for all that's wrong or might be wrong with your organization.

The solution to this problem is twofold: first, stick to your agenda and don't let yourself be derailed by those who would make your meetings a gripe session. Second, don't shut out the complainers altogether. Consider the scheduling of a separate meeting to air their concerns. These steps will keep your meetings more productive, while giving those with something negative to say a place and time to do so.

On the Witness Stand

22. *Don't let them rush you.* The witness stand is an uncomfortable place for most of us because we spend so little time there. To make matters worse, what you say can have far-reaching and sometimes devastating consequences.

As a corporate witness, your peers and superiors are likely to be watching. All this pressure and I haven't even mentioned the opposition yet. Of course, the opposition will want to increase the pressure by getting you to respond immediately to each question. You may be questioned by someone who shoots words at you like an automatic weapon, so you'll feel hurried and compelled to speak without thinking (which is just what the opposition wants you to do). Instead, pause before responding, even on easy questions. As you respond, speak deliberately and slowly. In this manner, you'll set a pattern to give yourself more think time for each response and also to mask your reaction as to the degree of ease or difficulty of each question.

23. *Greet silence with silence.* When a questioner wants a witness to say more, all he usually has to do is look directly at the witness at the end of the response and say nothing for a few seconds. Under the pressure of the moment, most witnesses will start talking again and often say things they wish they hadn't said. Remember, this extra verbiage was in response to silence. Now that you know this trick, don't become its victim.

24. *Just answer the questions.* Let your attorney win the case. Sometimes witnesses see themselves as soldiers on a field of battle, determined to lash out at the "enemy" at every opportunity. This is just how the opposition wants you to feel: combative, angry, aggressive, and, most of all, not thinking. With you in this emotional state, they'll have a much easier time getting you to say things you shouldn't. Instead of trying to win the case, concentrate on answering the questions truthfully and succinctly. Your attorney will do the strategizing and take the actions necessary to counter any problem testimony. Your role as a witness is just to answer the questions you are asked.

During a Crisis

25. *Maintain media contact at regular intervals.* During a crisis, the kind and degree of media coverage you receive will be a major component in shaping both the public perception of the severity of the crisis and your effectiveness in dealing with it. If you do not make yourself available, you increase the chance of building the

perception that you are avoiding coverage because you have something to hide, possibly your inability to manage the crisis. Part of
your communications plan in a crisis should be regularly scheduled
media briefings. Your public will get *your* story, rather than the mul-
titude of versions arrived at by reporters who did their investigating
without your input.

26. *Don't forget to talk to the troops.* Your employees will become
a major source of information in a crisis, not only for the media but
for anyone that they encounter outside the workplace. Facing constant inquiries as to what's happening at your company, as well as
the extra effort employees may have to make during a crisis, can be
tough on morale. Make your employees a top communications priority; they have a special stake in any crisis. As informed sources,
they can make good ambassadors as the public at large and the
media seek to find out what's going on. This reliance on employees
as communicators will boost morale, as well as provide reliable
information to those seeking it. It also will shut down the most
notorious and unreliable information center during any crisis—the
rumor mill.

27. *When a crisis is over, say so.* If you look at the history of corporate crises—be they financial, product related, or even crises of
public confidence—you will find that all of these situations had a
beginning, the particular event that precipitated the crisis; a middle
phase in which a crisis management plan was implemented; and
finally, an end, the phase in which business is getting back to normal. The problem is, if you don't declare an end to the crisis, the
public perception will persist that you are still mired in crisis and
that your products and services may somehow be affected. If the
crisis is severe enough, some people may even assume that you are
no longer in business. So, once a crisis has ended, be sure to declare
to all your constituents that the crisis is over and normalcy has
returned.

Summary

So, there you have it—twenty-seven quick fixes to help make you a more powerful communicator. Having taken you through hundreds of pages and tactics for all sorts of communicative encounters, I remain vividly aware that listeners and readers tend to remember what they hear (or read) last.

Therefore I want to encourage you at this closing moment not to be hypercritical of your abilities—as so many of you are. As I cautioned earlier, don't use the information contained in the preceding pages to give yourself a communicative makeover. Instead, accentuate and build on your strengths.

You may have come to realize that truly powerful communicators exude confidence, not by building an act, but by communicating with comfort and consistency, regardless of the situation or issues climate.

Consistency builds comfort, and that comfort communicates the confidence you need to achieve your full potential as a powerful and confident communicator.

Acknowledgments

Much of the information contained in this book is the result of discussions and interactions with my colleagues and students at John Jay College, as well as those in the corporate and government spheres with whom I've had the privilege of working. My thanks for all you have taught me!

Individual thanks go to my wife, Donna, for her unending love and encouragement; to my colleagues at John Jay including Jeremy Travis, Jane Bowers, Martin Wallenstein, Kathy Willis, and especially Blanche Cook for her cherished friendship and support; to Philip Turner at Sterling Publishing for his vision and guidance as well as to Iris Blasi, Brooke Barona, Chrissy Kwasnik, Rebecca Maines, and Isabel Stein for their superb efforts. Finally, to my friends Mike and Vicky Kay: thanks for listening.

Index

About the Author

Patrick Collins is president of Power Communication Strategies and has lectured and conducted seminars worldwide on presentation and media skills, witness preparation, negotiation, and many other communication topics. He is a Professor of Communications and a department chair at John Jay College of the City University of New York. Collins is the author of *Negotiate to Win!*, also available from Sterling Publishing Co., Inc.

Also Available

Negotiate to Win!
Talking Your Way to What You Want
by Patrick Collins

If you've ever walked away from a transaction feeling that someone got the better of you, or if you've ever said to yourself that there's no point in negotiating because "they'll only say no," then you have everything to gain from reading *Negotiate to Win!*

Negotiation is both an art and a science, with strategies you can master and people skills you can develop to get what you want on your own terms. Patrick Collins gets you started by revealing the Five Secrets of Successful Negotiators, citing guerilla tactics you can employ immediately, and suggesting situations where you can complete your basic training.

Next, it's time to tackle the biggest factor in all negotiations: people, from Tough Customers to Bullies. There are also tips on expertly managing negotiating environments, whether it's seating arrangements or the choice of room.

Once you are comfortable with the "negotiation mentality," delve into more advanced tactics. You'll learn when to stay silent, when to bluff, and how to find an opponent's "ouch point." Then discover how to recognize and counteract negotiation strategies that are being used against you, conduct cross-cultural negotiations, and break through impasses. Finally, Collins sums it all up with the Ten Commandments of Negotiation.

Negotiate to Win! offers the skills and confidence you need to gain the upper hand and attain the power to get more of what you want.

Sterling / 176 pages / ISBN 978-1-4027-6122-5 / $21.95 / January 2009
Available at fine bookstores everywhere
For more information, go to www.patrickjcollins.com.